THE 1986 TAX REFORM ACT

MAKING IT WORK FOR YOU

THE 1986 TAX REFORM ACT

MAKING IT WORK FOR YOU

Paul N. Strassels

The 1986 Tax Reform Act was signed into law October 22, 1986.

DOW JONES-IRWIN

Homewood, Illinois 60430

© Paul N. Strassels, 1987

All rights reserved. No part of this publication may be reproduced, stored in a retrieval system, or transmitted, in any form or by any means, electronic, mechanical, photocopying, recording, or otherwise, without the prior written permission of the publisher.

This publication is designed to provide accurate and authoritative information in regard to the subject matter covered. It is sold with the understanding that the publisher is not engaged in rendering legal, accounting, or other professional service. If legal advice or other expert assistance is required, the services of a competent professional person should be sought.

From a Declaration of Principles jointly adopted by a Committee of the American Bar Association and a Committee of Publishers.

ISBN 0-87094-935-7

Library of Congress Catalog Card No. 86–72444

Printed in the United States of America

4 5 6 7 8 9 0 VK 4 3 2 1 0 9 8 7

Introduction

The Tax Reform Act of 1986, agreed to in August, finally passed by Congress in September, and signed by President Reagan, is perhaps the most important piece of financial legislation to come out of Congress since 1913 when the 16th Amendment to the United States Constitution was ratified, authorizing the modern-day income tax. It has taken more than two years for everyone to come to agreement on the terms of this new tax law. For the most part, its provisions become effective January 1, 1987, although there are a number of important rules that become effective at other times, a few retroactively, but most prospectively.

NEW CONCEPTS FOR THE NATION'S TAX LAWS

The entire fabric of the Internal Revenue Code has been recut. Probably the most significant change is that the nation's income tax laws are no longer progressive in nature. Since the inception of this code, taxes have been assessed according to the ability of people to pay. The more you make, the more you should pay in tax. If you earn $20,000 a year, you should pay at an extremely low rate. When you make $75,000, you should pay at a higher rate. And when you make $250,000 a year, you should pay at an extremely high rate. But that's not the case any longer. When the new law is fully implemented, there will be only two rates, with a third reserved for taxpayers in only the highest income echelons.

What's more, Congress has also decided, along with removing the progressivity of the nation's tax rates, to end its long-standing policy of engineering (and manipulating) national social and economic change through the tax system. In the past, Congress has encouraged homeownership by allowing owners to deduct real estate taxes and interest on home mortgages. That policy is being continued. In the early 1980s, Congress decided it wanted to provide banks with a source of stable, long-term money that it could lend, and at the same time wanted to encourage individuals to save for retirement. The result was the Individual Retirement Account. It also wanted people to invest in real estate, oil and gas wells, mining operations, and farms, so it passed generous tax breaks to encourage people to sink their money in these investments. So they did.

But much of that philosophy has changed. Now if you want to invest in rental housing, for example, do so because you feel you'll earn a profit through appreciation, not because of the terrific tax benefits. Most are gone. If you want to be generous to your alma mater, do so out of a sense of pride and charity, not because of the tax write-offs. Chances are you won't get much.

Congress did a thorough job overhauling the nation's tax system. Tax rates have been slashed for individuals and businesses. Long-cherished tax breaks are gone. There's no more capital gains. The investment tax credit is scrapped. Both these tax breaks have been part of the federal income tax system for years (capital gains since 1921 and the investment credit since 1963). Depreciation deductions are revamped. The old favorite known as the Clifford trust is out, so you'll have to find other ways to finance college educations (there still are plenty of them, all perfectly legal). Tax shelter losses and consumer interest won't do you much good anymore. Individual Retirement Accounts are restricted, and contributions to company-run retirement plans are curtailed. All this change is due to the 1986 Tax Reform Act.

There's no question that the manner in which you conduct your personal, business, investment, retirement, and estate planning affairs will have to be thoroughly revised because of this historic legislation.

THE TAX REFORM ACT WAS A LONG TIME IN THE MAKING

The entire process started with public debate more than four years ago when the concept of a flat-tax, simple-tax was first being voiced as a viable alternative to the existing tax law.

There were three compelling reasons for the debate. First, there was the growing overall dissatisfaction of the general public with the terrible complexity of the tax law; second, a widespread underground economy developed that included many people who opted to drop out of the tax system by dealing only in cash; and third, there was a persistent widespread belief that the fat cats were avoiding income taxes entirely through irresponsible loopholes and preferences.

Washington politicians are smart people. They know a grass roots issue when they see one. That's precisely why many congressmen and senators took up the idea of tax reform, at one time or another, as their own. Then President Reagan adopted the idea of radical tax reform and made it one of his domestic priorities for his second term in office.

When he did, he insisted on only one important ingredient that he was not willing to set aside. He insisted that any legislation that eventually passed Congress had to be substantially revenue neutral. It could neither raise nor reduce the overall tax revenues taken in by the United States Treasury. Granted, some taxpayers would pay more tax, and others would pay less under the tax reform legislation. As with all tax revision bills, there would be winners and there would be losers. Nevertheless, President Reagan insisted that the tax bill couldn't raise or lower taxes, and if it did, he promised to veto it. He was not willing to compromise on this point.

THE TIMETABLE

Historically, tax legislation has been a maddeningly slow and tedious process, and this time was no different in that respect. Even when Congress finally decided that it would seriously approach the task of overhauling the nation's tax laws, it still took almost two years for legislators to settle on the form and substance of this tax law. During that time it was given up for dead on at least a half dozen occasions.

Debate first started in the tax-writing House Ways and Means Committee (that's where all federal tax legislation is required to begin) in early 1986. This tax-writing committee met for weeks, trying to sort through the various proposals before it. They heard testimony from every special interest group you can think of, as well as from the Treasury Department and others. Finally, after weeks of public hearings and private meetings, the politically powerful Chairman of the Ways and Means Committee, Dan Rostenkowski (D-Ill.), put together a package of proposals that met with the approval of a majority of Committee members.

Following procedures, Rostenkowski then sent the bill to the House floor so it could be debated by the full membership of the House of Representatives. After lengthy and often heated debate, the House agreed to its version of tax reform.

No one was particularly happy with what the House agreed to, not even the leadership in the House. In fact, at one point during the House's consideration of the legislation, it appeared as though the House leadership would not even let the pending tax bill come to a final vote. And even when it did, it only was passed because President Reagan promised that if the bill was sent to him in its current form (as passed by the House), he would not hesitate to veto it.

President Reagan reasoned that if the House failed in its attempt to pass at least some version of tax reform legislation, the Senate would never get a shot at it. (Tax bills can't originate in the Senate.) If the tax reform bill died in the House, all chances for reform would vanish, at least for the next few years.

The House of Representatives eventually passed its ideas for tax reform just before its Christmas recess and sent them to the Senate.

The Senate Finance Committee (the Senate's counterpart to the House Ways and Means Committee) got down to business soon after the first of the year (1986). As with most intricate tax legislation, the Senate had its own idea about what should be done to revise the nation's tax laws, and most of them were not included in the House's bill. They took the name of the House bill, and very little else. In essence, the Senate started from scratch.

Finance Committee Chairman Robert Packwood (R-Oregon) and his committee members held more hearings, met behind closed doors, talked with Treasury Department officials, lobbyists, and others, just like the House did. At this point, many special interest groups were successful in retaining their special tax breaks. The entire tax revision process begin to unravel. The special interest lobbyists loaded the bill down with one provision after another. The bill, as it stood in the Senate Finance Committee at this point, was terribly out of financial balance. The revenue drain was enormous. Senator Packwood was ready to scrap the entire exercise.

That's when he decided to try something unique. His ideas were radical. He met privately with a handful of trusted aides and other senators, and together they hammered out a thoroughly revolutionary approach to tax overhaul. The coalition he put together held firm against special interests. They decided to cut rates by more than half in many cases, eliminate long-time tax breaks, broaden the tax base by taxing previously untaxed income, and make certain that everyone with taxable income pays some tax by toughening the minimum tax rules.

The idea caught on like wildfire, both in the Senate and with the general taxpaying public. The perception was that this was a fairer way for everyone to pay their taxes. President Reagan added his support to the growing ground swell. By the time it finally came to a vote during the spring of 1986, the Finance Committee agreed unanimously to support Senator Packwood's bill, and after a great deal of debate on the Senate floor, the Senate voted overwhelmingly (97–3) for this version of tax reform.

ONE LAST STEP

Still, the process was not complete, not by a long shot. The House and Senate versions were vastly different, requiring a lengthy conference between the two legislative bodies. Packwood and Rostenkowski named members of their respective committees to meet and work out differences between the House and Senate bills. However, what finally happened was that only Rostenkowski and Packwood contributed to the conference in any meaningful way.

The key to the give-and-take during the weeks the Conference Committee chairmen debated the finer points of tax reform was that the bill had to remain revenue neutral. Both sides worked hard to maintain that balance, disagreeing only on who should have to pay what amount of tax. Finally they hammered out an agreement that both sides could live with. Today, the result is known as the Tax Reform Act of 1986.

We will all live with this newest tax legislation, but it may not be particularly easy. Few people are certain exactly what many of its provisions will mean in the long run. This much you can count on, however. You will have to revise your tax plans for 1986, 1987, and 1988, and I hope that this book will help.

Tax rates for 1987, 1988, and later years

You cannot effectively plan your taxes without easy access to the tax rate schedules. It's just not possible. You need to know at what levels your income will be taxed during the next few years, as you discover profitable ways to live without the benefits of capital gains, the IRA deduction, consumer interest, and more.

So here are the tax rates for 1987 and 1988 for single taxpayers, married couples filing jointly, and those filing as head of household. Also, individuals with substantial incomes need to know when they lose the benefits of the low 15 percent tax bracket and their personal exemptions. Those levels are listed below.

For single taxpayers filing for tax year 1987

The tax rate is	On taxable income of
11 percent	0–$ 1,800
15 percent	$ 1,800–$16,800
28 percent	$16,800–$27,000
35 percent	$27,000–$56,000
38.5 percent	Over $56,000

For married taxpayers filing jointly for tax year 1987

The tax rate is	On taxable income of
11 percent	0–$ 3,000
15 percent	$ 3,000–$28,000
28 percent	$28,000–$45,000
35 percent	$45,000–$90,000
38.5 percent	Over $90,000

For married couples filing separately for tax year 1987

Taxable income bracket amounts begin at one-half of the amounts for joint returns.

For heads of household filing for tax year 1987

The tax rate is	On taxable income of
11 percent	0–$ 2,600
15 percent	$ 2,600–$23,800
28 percent	$23,800–$38,300
35 percent	$38,300–$76,500
38.5 percent	Over $76,500

Maximum capital gains tax rate for all filers for tax year 1987 is 28 percent

For single taxpayers filing for 1988 and later tax years

The tax rate is	On taxable income of
15 percent	0–$17,850
28 percent	Over $17,850

For married taxpayers filing jointly for 1988 and later years

The tax rate is	On taxable income of
15 percent	0–$29,750
28 percent	Over $29,750

For married couples filing separately for 1988 and later years

Taxable income bracket amounts begin at one-half of the amounts used for joint returns.

For heads of household filing for 1988 and later years

The tax rate is	On taxable income of
15 percent	0–$25,300
28 percent	Over $25,300

Phaseout of 15 percent tax bracket in 1988

Once an individual's income reaches a certain level, Congress feels that the benefits of the 15 percent tax bracket should be phased out; a person earning $150,000 a year doesn't need the benefits of the 15 percent tax bracket on the first couple of thousand dollars he or she earns during the year. The phaseout of this tax break first becomes effective in 1988. What's more, it is indexed to reflect inflation, beginning in 1989.

For single taxpayers

For 1988 and later years, the benefits of the 15 percent tax bracket begin to be phased out for a single taxpayer once taxable income reaches $43,150. The phaseout is complete when income reaches $89,560.

For married taxpayers filing jointly

For 1988 and later years, the benefits of the 15 percent tax bracket begin to be phased out for a married couple filing jointly when taxable income reaches $71,900. The phaseout is complete when income reaches $149,250.

For married taxpayers filing separately

For 1988 and later years, the benefits of the 15 percent tax bracket begin to be phased out for married taxpayers filing separately when taxable income reaches $35,950. The phaseout is complete when income reaches $113,300.

For heads of household

For 1988 and later years, the benefits of the 15 percent tax bracket begin to be phased out for those using the head of household filing status when taxable income reaches $61,650. The phaseout is complete when income reaches $123,790.

Phaseout for personal exemptions

When personal incomes exceed the various ending levels set for the phaseout of the 15 percent tax bracket, the value of the personal exemption begins to erode.

For single taxpayers, the personal exemption is reduced when income exceeds $89,560.

For married couples filing jointly, the personal exemptions lose value when their income exceeds $149,250.

For married couples filing separately, the level is $113,300.

And for those utilizing the head of household tax status, they start to lose the personal exemption when income exceeds $123,790.

Contents

Introduction   v

Tax rates for 1987, 1988, and later years   xi

PART ONE   AN OVERVIEW   1

1   Individuals   3

Tax rates are slashed   3
The standard deduction is reinstated and improved   4
The personal exemption is almost doubled   4
Elderly and blind lose the extra personal exemption   5
The personal exemption and 15 percent tax rate are
    phased out for high-income taxpayers   5
Certain tax breaks are indexed to inflation   5
The two-earner deduction is repealed   5
Income averaging is gone, too   5
Unemployment benefits are fully taxed   5
Scholarships and fellowships are more harshly taxed   6
Awards and prizes are taxed   6
State and local sales taxes are no longer deductible; state
    and local Income, real estate, and property taxes are   6
Charitable deductions are available only to itemizers   7
Medical expense deductions will be hard to come by   7
Political contributions tax credit is repealed   7
Military and ministers keep their housing benefits   7

xv

Employee business expenses are tougher to take 7
New unreimbursed employee business expenses and moving expenses have a new status for deduction purposes 8
Miscellaneous itemized deductions will be less valuable 9
Consumer interest loses its luster 9
Mortgage interest on first and second homes is still deductible 9
There is still tax-deferral when you sell your personal residence 9
Casualty losses take a new twist 10
Overseas workers lose part of their exclusion 10
Self-employed workers get a break on their health insurance 10
Employee fringe benefits get a boost 10

2 Tax changes affecting your investments 11

Capital gains is repealed 11
The dividend exclusion is ended, too 12
Real estate investors take note of important changes 12
Rehabilitation expenditures still qualify for the tax credit 12
Real estate investment trusts escape change 13
Single premium whole life policies look good, too 13
The minimum tax provisions could be dangerous to the unwary 13
Life insurance paid in installments loses its appeal 14

3 Tax shelters 15

Tax shelters are defined, finally 15
The investment tax credit is repealed 16
Depreciation is not nearly as generous as it has been 16
Tax shelter losses are no longer deductible against wages 16
Real estate carries the same at-risk rules as other shelters 17

Tax shelter promoters and investors face stiffer
requirements   17

4   Tax-exempt bonds   19

Tax-exempt interest is less enticing   19
Tax-exempt interest will have to be reported to the IRS   20
Interest on most municipals stays tax-exempt, but some
will be taxed   20
Some tax-exempt interest may be subject to the minimum
tax   20

5   Retirement planning   21

IRAs are restricted beginning in 1987   21
Married couples lose out when only one is covered by a
company retirement plan   22
You can still make an IRA contribution regardless of
income   22
U.S. gold coins are okay for IRAs   22
Deferred compensation plans are more restricted by tax
reform   22
Hardship withdrawals from deferred compensation plans
are still permitted   23
SEP-IRAs should become popular   23
More workers than ever before will qualify for
pensions   23
You must start drawing your retirement by age 70 and one-
half   23
Ten-year forward averaging is cut by half   23
The special three-year rule for those who contribute to their
retirement fund is repealed   24

6   Family affairs   25

Trusts and estates will be taxed under a new tax rate
schedule   25
Trusts must pay estimated taxes   25

New Clifford Trusts and spousal remainder trusts are out   25
Income shifting takes on a whole new meaning   26
Children under age 14 are taxed differently than those age 14 or older   26

7   Business   29

Corporate tax rates are reduced   29
There's still no corporate deduction for dividend payouts   29
The dividends received deduction is reduced just a bit   29
The deduction for business meals is reduced by 20 percent   30
Business entertainment costs are only 80 percent deductible   30
Travel costs for business conventions are still okay   30
The investment tax credit is repealed, retroactively   30
Depreciation rules for property have been overhauled   30
Luxury cars receive special attention   31
The expensing deduction has been liberalized   31
Trademark and trade name costs will no longer be amortized over five years   31
Corporate capital gains rates are raised   31
The corporate minimum tax gets some teeth   32
Get ready for the accrual method of accounting   32
Most partnerships, S corporations, and personal service corporations will have to adopt the calendar year for tax purposes   32

8   Tougher compliance rules   33

There are four new penalties   33
You will pay the IRS more interest, but collect less   34
The IRS will receive more information reports on your financial activities   34
Tax shelter investors will be penalized further   35
Estimated taxes will have to be paid earlier   35

PART TWO THE SPECIFICS 37

9   Details for individuals 39

Personal tax rates are slashed 39
The standard deduction replaces the zero bracket amount 40
The personal exemption takes on new meaning 41
Two terrific deductions are gone, casualties of tax rate cuts 42
Unemployment compensation is fully taxable 43
Scholarships and fellowships are muddied 43
Awards and prizes are included in income 44
A number of personal tax breaks are repealed 45
Itemized deductions get a new look 49

10   Details for investors 55

The unkindest cut of all: Capital gains is gone 55
Depreciation is cut way back 58
Historic restoration 59
Minimum tax takes some careful watching 59
Take your life insurance proceeds and run 61
Real estate is hard hit by tax reform 61

11   Details on tax shelters 63

Tax shelters are defined 64
The investment tax credit is gone 64
Depreciation is not nearly as generous as it once was 65
The biggest change in tax shelters 66
Real estate 67

12   Details for tax-exempt bonds 69

Lower tax rates hurt tax-exempts 69
You will have to report your bond interest to the IRS 70
Most but not all municipals remain tax-exempt 72
The minimum tax bears watching 72

13 Details on retirement planning   75

Individual retirement accounts are not for everyone   76
U.S. gold and silver coins are fine for IRAs   80
Where you stick your IRA is important, too   80
Popular deferred compensation plans will still be the rage   81
SEP-IRAs should become popular as more employers install them   81
Vesting rights start earlier   81

14 Details on family and estate planning   83

Estates and trusts use a new tax rate schedule   83
Trusts and estates must pay quarterly estimated taxes   84
New trusts must use the calendar year   84
Clifford and spousal remainder trusts are out   85
Income shifting becomes superfluous   85

15 Details on new business rules   87

Corporate rates are cut for big business, but not for small; corporate capital gains rates are boosted   87
Still no deduction for dividends paid out   88
The dividends received deduction is cut, too   89
Business meals and entertainment expenses are only 80 percent deductible   89
Why small business is still the best play in town   89
The 10 percent investment tax credit is repealed   90
Expensing allowance has been doubled   90
Depreciation rules take another hit   91
Luxury cars is still a big issue   92
The corporate minimum tax gets tougher   92
A tough new accounting rule for small business   93

16 Details on new compliance rules   95

The IRS pays less interest, collects more   95
Big brother is watching   96

PART THREE BRAND NEW TAX SAVING OPPORTUNITIES 99

17 Year-end tax saving plans 101

    Accelerate your tax deductible expenses 102
    Delay income into later, lower-taxed years 105

18 Refinancing your mortgage 109

19 Planning divorce settlements 113

20 New retirement thinking 117

21 Self-employment tax advantages 125

22 Tax breaks that have not been repealed, and a few that have 131

23 New strategies for charitable giving 137

24 Assessing investment opportunities 143

    Capital gains—gone, but not forgotten 143
    Stocks and other equities 146
    Bonds 148
    Tax shelters are obsolete 149
    Real estate investment trusts 150
    Single premium whole life insurance 151
    U.S. treasury securities 152
    Series EE savings bonds 153
    Savings accounts 153

25 Real estate tax planning 155

Start your real estate empire with your own home 155
Landlords enjoy the best of both worlds 158
An important exception 159

Index 161

PART ONE ─────────────────────────

AN OVERVIEW

Here are the highlights of the Tax Reform Act of 1986. They are covered in more depth later in the book. But frequently people are in a hurry, and they want quick answers to their questions. If you only have time to quickly scan the latest changes in the tax law, look here first.

This portion of the book is broken down into various categories and subjects that taxpayers often identify with. There's a chapter that covers tax law changes for individuals, another for investments, for municipal bonds, and still others for tax shelters, real estate, the minimum tax, retirement planning, business, family planning, and even new compliance rules.

However, a caution is in order as you get ready to scan this portion of this book. The Tax Reform Act is both massive and comprehensive. The law itself runs close to 1,000 pages, and it will take years before the law is fully implemented. The committee reports discussing the various tax changes run equally as long. It will be years before the IRS gets through writing regulations explaining the details on each and every section of the new law. The new law adjusts literally hundreds of provisions in the tax law, perhaps even thousands. Each revision and amendment often has a profound impact on other rules that have not been revised by tax reform. For example, the standard deduction has been increased substantially and the tax rates have been slashed. That means fewer people will be itemizing their otherwise tax deductible expenses. And those who do will find their deductions much less valuable than before. The tightening of the rules on Individual Retirement Accounts (IRAs) will affect the manner in which you save toward retirement. Higher tax rates for high income people will affect the way divorce settlements are structured. Changes in trust rules mean you must find new ways to finance your children's college education.

No one can afford to ignore the impact of the 1986 Tax Reform Act. It's just too comprehensive, reaching into all aspects of a person's financial life.

1

Individuals

Individuals may be as profoundly affected as any taxpaying group. There are literally dozens of new rules to scan in order to be a net winner after tax reform.

TAX RATES ARE SLASHED

Beginning in 1987, there will be five tax rates for individuals.

For married couples filing jointly

The tax rate is	On taxable income of
11 percent	0–$ 3,000
15 percent	$ 3,000–$28,000
28 percent	$28,000–$45,000
35 percent	$45,000–$90,000
38.5 percent	Over $90,000

For single individuals

The tax rate is	On taxable income of
11 percent	0–$ 1,800
15 percent	$ 1,800–$16,800
28 percent	$16,800–$27,000
35 percent	$27,000–$54,000
38.5 percent	Over $54,000

For 1988, there will be only two rates:

For married couples filing jointly

The tax rate is	On taxable income of
15 percent	0–$29,750
28 percent	Over $29,750

For single taxpayers,

The tax rate is	On taxable income of
15 percent	0–$17,850
28 percent	Over $17,850

THE STANDARD DEDUCTION IS REINSTATED AND IMPROVED

For the past decade or so, taxpayers used a concept known as the zero bracket amount rather than the well-known standard deduction. They amount to one and the same thing. The zero bracket amount was built into the tax tables, so you didn't actually calculate your deduction on your tax return. Now we're back to the standard deduction, beginning in 1988. It amounts to $5,000 for married taxpayers filing jointly; $3,000 for a single taxpayer; and $2,500 for a married taxpayer filing separately. Beginning in 1989, the standard deduction will increase, based on inflation.

For 1987, the standard deduction will be the same amount as that of the zero bracket amount applied under the law before it was revised by the tax reform act: that works out to $3,760 for married couples filing jointly, $2,540 for singles and heads of household, and $1,880 for marrieds filing separately.

THE PERSONAL EXEMPTION IS ALMOST DOUBLED

In 1986, the personal exemption and the dependency exemption for each family member is $1,080. It jumps to $1,900 in 1987, $1,950 in 1988, and $2,000 in 1989 and later years. The personal exemption is another item that will be adjusted for inflation.

ELDERLY AND BLIND LOSE THE EXTRA PERSONAL EXEMPTION

The extra personal exemption available to those who have reached age 65 and/or are legally blind is repealed for 1987.

THE PERSONAL EXEMPTION AND 15 PERCENT TAX RATE ARE PHASED OUT FOR HIGH INCOME TAXPAYERS

Beginning in 1988, high income individuals stand to lose the twin benefits of the 15 percent tax bracket and the $1,950 personal exemption. For married taxpayers, these benefits begin to be phased out once income reaches $71,900. For single taxpayers, the phaseout begins at $43,150.

CERTAIN TAX BREAKS ARE INDEXED TO INFLATION

Every year, the tax brackets, personal exemption, and standard deduction will be adjusted to reflect inflation. Uneven amounts will be rounded down to the nearest $50. Inflation will be measured every twelve months, ending each September 30.

THE TWO-EARNER DEDUCTION IS REPEALED

After 1986, the 10 percent deduction for the smaller income of two-earner couples is repealed. The maximum deduction in 1986 is 10 percent of the smaller income or $3,000, whichever is less.

INCOME AVERAGING IS GONE, TOO

After 1986, income averaging is repealed. You can no longer save on your taxes for a terrific year after suffering through a couple of so-so years.

UNEMPLOYMENT BENEFITS ARE FULLY TAXED

Beginning in 1987, all unemployment benefits will be fully taxed. Through 1986, some or all of these benefits are tax exempt, the amount depending on the amount of your other income.

SCHOLARSHIPS AND FELLOWSHIPS ARE MORE HARSHLY TAXED

Only scholarship and fellowship grants spent by degree candidates on tuition and course-related equipment will be excluded from income. What's spent on room, board, and other expenses will have to be included in the student's income. This change affects grants made after September 25, 1985. Even those receiving federal grants will have to pay tax on the money they receive.

AWARDS AND PRIZES ARE TAXED

Win a prize or an award for charitable, scientific, or artistic achievement and you'll have to pay tax on it unless, of course, you decide to assign it to a charitable or similar organization.

There is still a limited exclusion from tax for awards made to employees for length of service and safety. All other employment awards and prizes are taxable, except for extremely small items.

STATE AND LOCAL SALES TAXES ARE NO LONGER DEDUCTIBLE; STATE AND LOCAL INCOME, REAL ESTATE, AND PROPERTY TAXES ARE

Beginning in 1987, the itemized deduction that individuals have taken for state and local sales taxes is repealed.

Sales taxes paid by businesses in buying and selling property and investments are not deductible, but rather are added to the price of the property.

The deduction for state and local income taxes, real estate taxes, and personal property taxes is still available to those who itemize their deductions.

CHARITABLE DEDUCTIONS ARE AVAILABLE ONLY TO ITEMIZERS

The year 1986 is the last that individuals who do not itemize their charitable donations can benefit from their own generosity. Beginning in 1987, only those who itemize their deductions will be able to write off their charitable donations.

MEDICAL EXPENSE DEDUCTIONS WILL BE HARD TO COME BY

Beginning in 1987, only medical expenses that exceed 7.5 percent of your adjusted gross income will be tax deductible.

There is one break for medical expenditures. The cost of adapting your personal residence to meet the needs of a handicapped individual may qualify for the medical deduction.

POLITICAL CONTRIBUTIONS TAX CREDIT IS REPEALED

Beginning in 1987, you will no longer be able to take a tax credit for political contributions.

MILITARY AND MINISTERS KEEP THEIR HOUSING BENEFITS

Over the IRS's objections, military personnel and the clergy can continue to deduct the amount of mortgage interest and real estate tax they pay, despite the fact they receive tax-free housing allowances.

EMPLOYEE BUSINESS EXPENSES ARE TOUGHER TO TAKE

The new 80-percent rule

Only 80 percent of your otherwise tax deductible business meals and entertainment expenses can be deducted from your income, as opposed to 1986's 100 percent. There is a narrow exception for most banquet meeting meals.

If you are reimbursed by your employer for what you spend on business meals and entertainment, the 80-percent rule does not apply. It is your employer that will be subject to the 80-percent rule. Also, to get any deduction, you will have to prove who was entertained, the business purpose, and so on, just as always; so keep good records.

Investment seminars are out

Beginning in 1987, only the costs associated with attending seminars, conventions, and meetings that are directly related to your trade or business will be deductible. Investment and education seminars are out.

Educational travel is not deductible

You can no longer write off the cost of educational travel.

Charitable travel is restricted

You can still deduct the cost of traveling for a charity, but only when there is no significant level of personal recreation or vacation involved. In other words, you will not be able to tack on a personal vacation to a trip you undertook for a charitable organization.

UNREIMBURSED EMPLOYEE BUSINESS EXPENSES AND MOVING EXPENSES HAVE A NEW STATUS FOR TAX DEDUCTION PURPOSES

Unreimbursed employee business expenses will be taken as an itemized deduction beginning in 1987, rather than as an adjustment to income, as in earlier years.

Similarly, moving expenses will have to be taken as an itemized deduction by employees and self-employed individuals who incur costs for work-related moves.

MISCELLANEOUS ITEMIZED DEDUCTIONS WILL BE LESS VALUABLE

In fact, they may be nonexistent. Beginning in 1987, miscellaneous itemized deductions will be deductible only to the extent they exceed 2 percent of your adjusted gross income. That includes unreimbursed employee business expenses, union dues, safety deposit box rentals, work clothing, employment agency fees, job hunting expenses, and the like.

CONSUMER INTEREST LOSES ITS LUSTER

The interest you pay on credit card balances, car loans, and other installment debts will be 100 percent deductible in 1986, only 65 percent deductible in 1987, 40 percent in 1988, 20 percent in 1989, and 10 percent in 1990. After that the deduction for consumer interest is repealed.

MORTGAGE INTEREST ON FIRST AND SECOND HOMES IS STILL DEDUCTIBLE

Congress spared the deduction for the interest you pay on the mortgage loan covering your primary personal residence as well as for a second or vacation home.

THERE IS STILL TAX-DEFERRAL WHEN YOU SELL YOUR PERSONAL RESIDENCE

Many people have worried about this, so the good news is, there is no news. When you sell your personal residence at a profit and replace it with a more expensive place within two years, you still do not pay tax on your profits. The tax is deferred. That's true whether you put the profit into the new house or use it for other purposes.

For those who have passed their 55th birthday, you can still pocket as much as $125,000 of the profit from the sale of your personal residence, tax-free. Again, there is no change from the old law.

CASUALTY LOSSES TAKE A NEW TWIST

Casualty losses are tax deductible as itemized expenses only to the extent they exceed 10 percent of your adjusted gross income. What's more, you now must make a claim against your insurance if you have coverage. Previously, you could decide against making an insurance claim if you wanted.

OVERSEAS WORKERS LOSE PART OF THEIR EXCLUSION

The maximum annual exclusion for foreign income earned by Americans working overseas drops by $10,000, to $70,000 beginning in 1987.

SELF-EMPLOYED WORKERS GET A BREAK ON THEIR HEALTH INSURANCE

Beginning in 1987, 25 percent of the health insurance premiums paid by self-employed individuals to cover themselves and their family is tax deductible.

EMPLOYEE FRINGE BENEFITS GET A BOOST

Group legal and educational assistance plans get new life, at least through the end of 1987. Amounts paid on behalf of workers are not included in the employees' incomes.

2

Tax changes affecting your investments

The Tax Reform Act has done more to change the way you think about investments than any other law in history, if only because the overall tax rates are slashed. The following is a summary of many of the most important provisions.

CAPITAL GAINS IS REPEALED

Beginning in 1987, investors will no longer exclude 60 percent of the profit from the sale of an investment they have held for more than six months. At that time, investment profits will be treated just like any other type of income—they will be fully taxed. The distinction between long-term and short-term investments will no longer be important. Losses on the sale of investments will be used to offset profits.

Net profits will be fully taxed. Net losses will be deductible up to $3,000 a year. Excess amounts will be carried over to future years.

The maximum tax rate on investment profits for 1986 is 20 percent. For 1987, it will be 28 percent. And in 1988 and later years, the top rate may be even higher for well-to-do taxpayers who find their 15 percent tax bracket and personal exemption tax breaks phased out as their incomes increase.

THE DIVIDEND EXCLUSION IS ENDED, TOO

After 1986, an investor can no longer exclude the first $100 of dividend income ($200 for married couples filing jointly).

REAL ESTATE INVESTORS TAKE NOTE OF IMPORTANT CHANGES

The depreciation schedule for residential housing newly placed in service is 27.5 years, as opposed to 19 years. Accelerated depreciation is out; straight-line depreciation is in.

The depreciation schedule for nonresidential real estate is 31.5 years, again using a straight-line rather than accelerated schedule.

Keep in mind, however, that real estate previously placed in service will retain the depreciation schedule first used when you acquired the property. If you bought the property in 1981, for example, you would continue to use the 15-year accelerated depreciation system you've been using for the past half decade.

Real estate activities are now considered passive investments rather than active ones. That means net real estate losses are treated just like losses from tax sheltered investments. Losses are not deductible against salary and other income, but rather can only be offset against passive income. Unused losses can be recouped when the property is sold.

There is an exception for small residential real estate investors with incomes below $100,000. If you actively manage your residential real estate, you can deduct up to $25,000 a year in net losses from these activities. You begin to lose the deduction as your income increases to $150,000, at which level no deduction is permitted.

REHABILITATION EXPENDITURES STILL QUALIFY FOR THE TAX CREDIT

You can claim a 10 percent tax credit for qualified expenditures incurred while rehabilitating a building (other than a certified historic structure) built before 1936. You get a 20 percent tax credit for expenses you have while rebuilding a certified historic structure.

REAL ESTATE INVESTMENT TRUSTS ESCAPE CHANGE

Investments in REITs look good right now. The tax rules affecting real estate investment trusts were not changed by tax reform to any great extent. In fact, the few changes that were made will serve to enhance this investment.

SINGLE PREMIUM WHOLE LIFE POLICIES LOOK GOOD, TOO

Again, the tax law did not change the ground rules on single premium whole life policies. In fact, they may prove to be a better deal over the long haul than an IRA, if only because you are not limited on the amount you can put into a policy; and, just like an IRA, the dividends and interest accumulate tax-deferred.

THE MINIMUM TAX PROVISIONS COULD BE DANGEROUS TO THE UNWARY

The alternative minimum tax, set at 20 percent in 1986, is assessed on taxpayers who have been largely successful in cutting their taxes down to next to nothing. It is intended to make certain that everyone pays something to support the government, no matter how successful their tax planning. You compute your taxes under the regular rules, and then again under the rules for the alternative minimum tax. You are to pay the larger of the two bills.

The minimum tax is assessed on items of tax preference such as the untaxed portion of long-term capital gains, stock options, and accelerated depreciation, among others.

Beginning in 1987, the alternative minimum tax rate is raised to 21 percent.

The amount of income that is exempted from the minimum tax is $40,000 for married couples filing jointly,

$30,000 for single taxpayers, and $20,000 for couples filing separately. This exemption is phased out at a rate of 25 cents on the dollar as income increases above $150,000 for married taxpayers, and $112,500 for singles.

LIFE INSURANCE PAID IN INSTALLMENTS LOSES ITS APPEAL

Prior to tax reform, a surviving spouse who received periodic payments from life insurance was allowed to exclude the first $1,000 worth of interest earned on those funds and paid to him or her during the year. Now, that $1,000 exclusion is ended for beneficiaries of policies covering deaths that occur after the date the Tax Reform Act was enacted.

3

Tax shelters

What Congress gives, Congress can take away. And that is precisely what has happened to tax sheltered investments. Over the past decade or so, Congress has encouraged certain types of investments by providing excellent tax benefits for those who would finance them. On the one hand, critics of these investments often viewed the tax benefits as outrageous, arguing that the revenue drain was not worth the benefits provided to society. A perfect example is the overbuilding binge in real estate, fueled exclusively by the valuable tax benefits available to investors. On the other hand, investors viewed these tax benefits as nothing more than preferences encouraged by Congressional tax writers, and they took advantage of them in droves.

But that's all over. The heyday of deep tax sheltered investments is gone. Congress has taken away the tax benefits. Here is specifically what has happened.

TAX SHELTERS ARE DEFINED, FINALLY

A tax shelter is defined as an investment where the ratio of the deductions plus 300 percent of the tax credits to the cash you actually invest is projected to be more than two to one. Steeper shelters will cause difficulty for investors and the IRS.

THE INVESTMENT TAX CREDIT IS REPEALED

It was the exceedingly generous Investment Tax Credit (ITC) that made many tax sheltered investments work. Without the credit, the numbers fall apart.

DEPRECIATION IS NOT NEARLY AS GENEROUS AS IT HAS BEEN

Along with the repeal of the ITC, Congress tightened up on depreciation deductions. Commerical real estate, for example, cannot be written off over 15, 18, or 19 years as in recent years, but rather over 31.5 years. What's more, when it comes to writing off real estate, depreciation will be computed under the less advantageous straight-line system, rather than under the faster accelerated methods.

TAX SHELTER LOSSES ARE NO LONGER DEDUCTIBLE AGAINST WAGES

Perhaps the biggest change to emerge in the area of tax sheltered investments is the new prohibition against offsetting tax shelter losses against regularly taxed income.

In years past, an investor in a three-to-one shelter could invest $10,000 and find himself entitled to $30,000 worth of deductions. That $30,000 was used to offset income—wages, dividends, interest, and the like. He would receive a tax benefit of much more than the $10,000 he originally invested. As a result, he didn't much care whether or not the investment ever turned a profit. He had already made out very nicely.

Tax shelters are considered "passive" investments, as are rental activities. Stock market activities are considered active investments, even though you might turn over your entire portfolio to a broker for handling.

Losses from passive investments are not deductible against regular income or against profits from "active" investments. You cannot offset shelter losses against stock market gains. The only way to enjoy a benefit from losses on passive investments is to offset them against profits from passive investments. That means you need to seek out limited partnerships that earn a profit.

There is an exception worth noting. Net losses from tax shelters purchased on or before the date of enactment will be fully deductible on your 1986 tax return, 65 percent deductible in 1987, 40 percent deductible in 1988, 20 percent deductible in 1989, and 10 percent deductible in 1990. In 1991 and later years, none of the losses will be deducted, but rather will have to be offset against passive income, or carried forward to future years.

Losses from limited partnerships purchased after enactment will not qualify for the limited deduction, but will have to be either offset or carried forward immediately.

REAL ESTATE CARRIES THE SAME AT-RISK RULES AS OTHER SHELTERS

In almost every case, the same at-risk limitations that have long applied to investments in oil and gas properties, mining operations, and other shelters will now extend to real estate investments.

TAX SHELTER PROMOTERS AND INVESTORS FACE STIFFER REQUIREMENTS

Promoters will have to register their investments with the IRS. If they don't, there's a new penalty amounting to one percent of the amount invested in the shelter, without exception. If investors fail to report the tax shelter ID number on their tax returns when they file, there will be a $250 fine, up from $50. Promoters who fail to maintain a list of investors could be fined $50 per missing name, up to a maximum fine of $100,000.

4

Tax-exempt bonds

Many people today are questioning the wisdom of keeping their money tied up in tax-exempt municipal bonds when the maximum tax rate for individuals will drop from a high of 50 percent in 1986, all the way down to 38.5 in 1987, and 28 percent in 1988.

Prior to tax overhaul with its cut in tax rates, tax-exempts were a good choice for investors in the upper income tax brackets. Say you had a choice between a 12 percent taxable bond and a 6.5 percent tax-exempt. Assuming you were in the 50 percent tax bracket, the tax-exempt was the better deal. You needed a 13 percent return on the taxable bond to be in as good a position as you were with a 6.5 tax-exempt bond.

Today, the equation has changed somewhat. You may be better off going with a fully-taxable rather than a tax-exempt bond. It all depends on the after-tax yield. The new law didn't make extensive changes in the taxation of municipal bonds, but the few changes that it did make are quite important, nonetheless.

TAX-EXEMPT INTEREST IS LESS ENTICING

When the IRS was taking 50 cents on the dollar, tax-exempt interest was a valuable commodity. Now, with the IRS getting only 28 cents on each dollar of interest, municipals lose some of their luster. Whether or not tax-exempt municipal bonds are an attractive investment for you all depends on what other investments in today's financial markets are paying.

TAX-EXEMPT INTEREST WILL HAVE TO BE REPORTED TO THE IRS

The IRS will add a new line to your tax return for you to report any tax-exempt interest income you collect during the year. There won't be any tax imposed, but don't be surprised if the IRS someday asks where you got the money to buy the tax-exempt bonds in the first place.

INTEREST ON MOST MUNICIPALS STAYS TAX-EXEMPT, BUT SOME WILL BE TAXED

Interest paid to you on all tax-exempt bonds issued before September 1, 1986 remains tax-exempt. Interest paid to you on all bonds issued by state and local governmental entities remains tax-exempt regardless when they were issued.

Interest on newly-issued bonds that actually provide financing for nongovernmental units (these are called private activity bonds) is taxable unless there is a specific exception provided for it. That means the interest paid on bond issues used to finance most sports arenas, stadiums, and the like, will be taxed. Check with your broker on the tax status of private activity bonds before buying.

SOME TAX-EXEMPT INTEREST MAY BE SUBJECT TO THE MINIMUM TAX

Congress has included, as an item of tax preference that will be subject ot the individual minimum tax, the amount of tax-exempt interest you collect from newly-issued private activity bonds.

5

Retirement planning

The rules have been changed in the middle of the game. You may have been saving toward retirement with an Individual Retirement Account (IRA) since the early 1980's, counting on it to supplement your retirement nest egg. You may have been salting away funds through your employer's retirement plan, or using the 401(k) plan at work, or funding a self-employed Keogh retirement plan.

But because of tax reform, you need to rethink your retirement plans. Some of the rules that have changed will hurt you, while others will definitely help. Here's a rundown.

IRAs ARE RESTRICTED BEGINNING IN 1987

If you are not covered by a company-sponsored retirement plan, you can still fund your IRA and deduct your contribution.

If you are covered by a company retirement plan and are single, you can still fund and deduct your IRA contribution as long as your income is under $25,000 a year.

If you are covered by a company retirement plan and are single, you can deduct a portion of your IRA contribution when your income falls between $25,000 and $35,000.

If you are covered by a company retirement plan and are single, you cannot deduct any portion of your IRA contribution when your income exceeds $35,000.

If you are covered by a company retirement plan and you are married, you can still fund and deduct your IRA contribution as long as your family income is under $40,000 a year.

If you are covered by a company plan and are married, you can deduct only a portion of your IRA contribution when your income falls between $40,000 and $50,000.

If you are covered by a company plan and are married, you cannot deduct any portion of your IRA contribution when your income exceeds $50,000.

MARRIED COUPLES LOSE OUT WHEN ONLY ONE IS COVERED BY A COMPANY RETIREMENT PLAN

If one partner is covered by a company retirement plan, the other is also considered to be covered for IRA deduction purposes.

YOU CAN STILL MAKE AN IRA CONTRIBUTION REGARDLESS OF INCOME

Even though you may not be allowed to deduct your IRA contribution because you are covered by a company plan and your income exceeds the levels specificed for single or married taxpayers, you can still make an IRA contribution for the year. It must not exceed $2,000. While the contribution is not deductible, the dividends and interest earned on the funds will accumulate tax-deferred.

U.S. GOLD COINS ARE OKAY FOR IRAs

If you don't like CDs or mutual funds for your IRA, you are now allowed to buy U.S. gold and silver coins for your retirement account. Other collectibles are still out-of-bounds for IRAs.

DEFERRED COMPENSATION PLANS ARE MORE RESTRICTED BY TAX REFORM

Beginning next year, the most you as an employee can elect to sink into a deferred compensation arrangement (like a 401(k) plan) is $7,000 annually.

HARDSHIP WITHDRAWALS FROM DEFERRED COMPENSATION PLANS ARE STILL PERMITTED

You can make hardship withdrawals from your deferred compensation plan, but only up to the amount of your elective contributions.

SEP-IRAs SHOULD BECOME POPULAR

Employees can make elective contributions to their employer's Simplified Employee Plan-IRA (SEP-IRA) up to $7,000 a year. But if you make an SEP-IRA contribution, you cannot make a tax-deductible personal IRA contribution.

MORE WORKERS THAN EVER BEFORE WILL QUALIFY FOR PENSIONS

Employer-sponsored retirement plans will provide vested (guaranteed) benefits to workers under one of two schedules: either workers will be fully vested after five years on the job, or 20 percent of their benefits will vest each year after three years on the job. In the second situation, workers will receive vested retirement benefits earlier, and full benefits later.

YOU MUST START DRAWING YOUR RETIREMENT BY AGE 70 AND ONE-HALF

You must start withdrawing funds (from your tax-sheltered annuities, tax-qualified retirement plans, and IRAs by a date no later than April 1 of the year after that in which you reach age 70 and one-half.

TEN-YEAR FORWARD AVERAGING IS CUT BY HALF

Those receiving a lump-sum distribution from their retirement plan will still have a choice. They can either roll the money over into an IRA, or they can pay tax on what they get. To help ease the immediate tax bite, they can utilize what's known as "forward averaging." Under old law, they used ten-year forward averaging. New law cuts it down to five years.

THE SPECIAL THREE-YEAR RULE FOR THOSE WHO CONTRIBUTE TO THEIR RETIREMENT FUND IS REPEALED

This special rule primarily affects government workers who help fund their retirement. Under the old law, you would not be taxed on your retirement pension until after you recouped your contribution, as long as that took three years or less. That three-year rule is repealed. Now each pension check will be part income and part return of capital.

6

Family affairs

Savvy financial planners have long utilized the many tax advantages allowed by law. They've set up income splitting strategies between low-income children and high-income parents. They've used Clifford and spousal remainder trusts, gift programs, and more. The idea behind the exercise was to keep more of the family money in the family by legally sending less of it to the IRS. However, because of changes to the tax laws, many long-time, tax-saving strategies will no longer work.

TRUSTS AND ESTATES WILL BE TAXED UNDER A NEW TAX RATE SCHEDULE

Estates and trusts will pay at a rate of 15 percent on the first $5,000 of taxable income. Excess income is taxed at 28 percent. The benefit of the 15 percent tax rate is phased out as income increases from $13,000 to $26,000.

TRUSTS MUST PAY ESTIMATED TAXES

Trusts will now be treated just like individuals when it comes to paying quarterly estimated taxes.

NEW CLIFFORD TRUSTS AND SPOUSAL REMAINDER TRUSTS ARE OUT

Grantors would fund these trusts with income-producing assets, and name a child as beneficiary for a set number of years. After the time had elapsed, the trust assets would revert to the grantor. In the meantime, the income would be taxed to the low-tax-bracketed child, rather than the high-income parent.

But no longer. The law now says that the income generated by a trust will be taxed to the grantor (parent). Clifford and spousal trusts no longer work.

Fortunately, there are two exceptions. First, the trust stands when the assets revert to the grantor after the death of the beneficiary, so long as that person is a lineal descendant. Second, pre-existing Clifford and spousal remainder trusts retain their old status so long as they were set up prior to March 1, 1986. Also, you cannot transfer additional assets to a pre-existing trust.

INCOME SHIFTING TAKES ON A WHOLE NEW MEANING

Since parents will pay no more than 28 percent of their income in tax, beginning in 1988 (38.5 percent in 1987), the amount of tax saved by shifting income from a parent to a child is severely diminished. When you could shift personal income that would have been taxed at 50 percent to a child who was taxed at 14 percent, the savings were substantial. That's no longer the case.

CHILDREN UNDER AGE 14 ARE TAXED DIFFERENTLY THAN THOSE AGE 14 OR OLDER

A child who receives unearned income (that is dividends, interest, rents, royalties, etc., but not wages) from assets given by parents, will be taxed at the top tax rate of his or her parents.

Fortunately, there are still three exceptions. First, if the child is age 14 or older, his income will be taxed to him. Period. The general rule just mentioned does not apply.

Second, even if the child is under 14, he gets the first $1,000 taxed to him in his low tax bracket. Only amounts in excess of $1,000 are taxed as if they were in the parent's high bracket.

And third, this rule only applies to unearned income. Wages and salaries earned by a youngster will be taxed at the child's income tax bracket, not the parent's.

7

Business

The Tax Reform Act has been touted as a tax cut for individuals. That's true. Overall, individuals receive most of the benefits of this tax overhaul. However, when taxes are reduced for individual taxpayers, businesses are called on to make up the difference. That's certainly the case with this tax reform effort. Businesses and business people will learn to live with a revised set of tax rules. It won't be particularly easy, but the sooner you get on track, the better off you will be. Here are the highlights of what the Tax Reform Act of 1986 has done to business.

CORPORATE TAX RATES ARE REDUCED

Effective July 1, 1987, the top corporate tax rate drops to 34 percent. That's down from 46 percent.

THERE'S STILL NO CORPORATE DEDUCTION FOR DIVIDEND PAYOUTS

There had been talk of permitting corporations a partial deduction for dividends paid to shareholders. That never came to pass.

THE DIVIDENDS RECEIVED DEDUCTION IS REDUCED JUST A BIT

The 85 percent deduction that corporations get on dividends they receive from investments in other corporations' stock is reduced to 80 percent beginning in 1987.

THE DEDUCTION FOR BUSINESS MEALS IS REDUCED BY 20 PERCENT

Only 80 percent of the cost of business meals will be tax deductible. That means 80 percent of the cost of the meal, tip, and tax. This includes meals eaten while on the road as well as those furnished at the office; plus business has to be discussed either during, before, or after the meal. The discussion rule is waived when you are on the road eating alone.

BUSINESS ENTERTAINMENT COSTS ARE ONLY 80 PERCENT DEDUCTIBLE

As with business meals, business entertainment costs will only be 80 percent deductible.

TRAVEL COSTS FOR BUSINESS CONVENTIONS ARE STILL OKAY

Contrary to many reports, businesses will still be allowed to fully deduct the travel costs associated with attending conventions, meetings, and seminars that are directly related to their trades and businesses. Travel costs of investment seminars are no longer deductible, beginning in 1987.

THE INVESTMENT TAX CREDIT IS REPEALED, RETROACTIVELY

Effective January 1, 1986, the Investment Tax Credit (ITC) is repealed. No longer can businesses write off up to 10 percent of the cost of machinery, cars, and the like directly against their tax liability.

DEPRECIATION RULES FOR PROPERTY HAVE BEEN OVERHAULED

These new rules will apply to property placed in service on or after January 1, 1987.

The new depreciation system lists eight classifications for business property. Class lives run from a low of three years to a high of 31.5 years. What's more, there are special types of property with lives running as long as 50 years.

Cars and trucks will have a five-year useful life for depreciation purposes and be depreciated using the 200 percent declining balance method.

Residential real estate will be depreciated over 27.5 years using the straight-line method.

Commercial real estate will be depreciated over 31.5 years, once again using the straight-line method.

LUXURY CARS RECEIVE SPECIAL ATTENTION

The maximum first-year depreciation allowance for a business car is $2,560, $4,100 for the second year, $2,450 for the third year, and $1,475 for each succeeding year.

THE EXPENSING DEDUCTION HAS BEEN LIBERALIZED

Instead of forcing businesses to depreciate each and every piece of business property, the law calls for a $10,000 allowance for taxpayers who purchase depreciable business property. That means you can almost write off the price of a relatively inexpensive business vehicle. The allowance phases out when you buy more than $200,000 worth of tangible personal property in a year.

TRADEMARK AND TRADE NAME COSTS WILL NO LONGER BE AMORTIZED OVER FIVE YEARS

The new law revokes the election to amortize the costs incurred while obtaining trademarks and trade names for the business.

CORPORATE CAPITAL GAINS RATES ARE RAISED

While personal capital gains rates are raised to 28 percent in 1987 and 33 percent in 1988, the new corporate capital gains rate is 34 percent. That's the rate a corporation will pay on the profitable sale of an investment.

THE CORPORATE MINIMUM TAX GETS SOME TEETH

There are new corporate minimum tax rules that will nab some corporations that would not otherwise pay any corporate tax. If your corporation pays less than 20 percent of its taxable income to the IRS, you'll have to become familiar with the details of the corporate minimum tax.

GET READY FOR THE ACCRUAL METHOD OF ACCOUNTING

Unless your annual gross receipts are $5 million or less, you will most likely have to convert your corporate books from the cash method of accounting to the accrual method. This applies to all regular corporations, a partnership that has a regular corporation as a partner, and tax-exempt trusts that earn unrelated business income. Farmers and personal service corporations may qualify for an exception.

MOST PARTNERSHIPS, S CORPORATIONS, AND PERSONAL SERVICE CORPORATIONS WILL HAVE TO ADOPT THE CALENDAR YEAR FOR TAX PURPOSES

Beginning in 1987, most partnerships, S corporations, and personal service corporations will have to adopt the calendar year as their own for income tax reporting purposes, unless they get a waiver from the IRS. That's unlikely because the IRS has wanted this rule for some time. If your business uses other than the calendar year, you should visit with your accountant as quickly as you can get the appointment.

8

Tough compliance rules

An important part of the tax reform plan was to maintain revenues and expenditures in relative balance. Whenever a congressman or senator wanted to add a tax preference to the bill that would wind up costing the government some revenue, he had to come up with a corresponding provision that would replace the money his proposal would cost.

One relatively painless technique that Congress used to generate much-needed funds to keep the bill in balance was to enlist the aid of the Internal Revenue Service. Congress has given the IRS a much stronger hand to enforce the nation's tax laws by passing a number of tough compliance measures. You'll have to learn to live with them, and hopefully sidestep the worst of the bunch.

THERE ARE FOUR NEW PENALTIES

Penalties are an easy way to collect money without voting new taxes.

There's a new penalty for faulty information returns

The maximum penalty for failure to file an information return with the IRS and furnish a copy to a taxpayer jumps to $100,000 for each category of filing. The penalty for each omission is $50. Plus, there is a new $5 penalty for failure to correct an erroneous information return.

The penalty for failure to pay is tougher under new law

The penalty for failure to pay your taxes is doubled from one-half percent to a full one percent, up to a maximum penalty of 25 percent.

Avoid costly negligence and fraud penalties

The IRS will not try to collect the 5 percent negligence penalty when it goes after a fraud penalty based on the omission of the same income.

The IRS will assess a negligence penalty whenever a person fails to report income that is the subject of an information return. It used to be that only unreported dividend and interest income was subject to the penalty.

The fraud penalty will only be applied to that portion of an underpayment that is attributable to fraud. However, that fraud penalty is increased to 75 percent.

The 10 percent penalty for the substantial understatement of your tax liability is doubled to 20 percent.

YOU WILL PAY IRS MORE INTEREST, BUT COLLECT LESS

The interest rate you must pay on tax deficiencies will be one percentage point higher than the rate that the IRS must pay on tax overpayments. What's more, the interest rate will be redetermined quarterly instead of semiannually.

THE IRS WILL RECEIVE MORE INFORMATION REPORTS ON YOUR FINANCIAL ACTIVITIES

Those who pay you money will comply with IRS requirements because if they don't, they will be roundly penalized. And if you don't report the income you should, you, too, will be saddled with negligence and other penalties, or worse.

The IRS will hear of real estate transactions

Beginning in 1987, real estate transactions will have to be reported to the IRS. Usually the settlement attorney or other person responsible for closing will send the information to the IRS. But if they fail, the responsibility falls to the lender and brokers involved.

The government will tell the IRS if you have a federal contract

For all new federal contracts, as well as those in effect January 1, 1987, the executive agency will file an information return detailing your financial dealings.

Royalty payments will now be reported

Youngsters' social security numbers will be listed

Parents will have to list on their tax returns the social security numbers of their tax dependents who are five years old or older.

Tax-exempt interest will have to be reported, but won't be taxed

Beginning in 1987, the IRS will provide a place on your tax return for you to report all tax-exempt interest you received during the year.

TAX SHELTER INVESTORS WILL BE PENALIZED FURTHER

Underpayments of tax resulting from a sham tax shelter will be subject to a 120 percent interest charge.

ESTIMATED TAXES WILL HAVE TO BE PAID EARLIER

Beginning in 1987, individuals will have to pay 90 percent (instead of 80 percent) of their current year's tax liability to avoid the underpayment of estimated tax penalty.

PART TWO

THE SPECIFICS

The first part of this book presented an overview of the Tax Reform Act of 1986. That overview is just the skeleton. It's only the headlines. There's more—much more—to this newest set of tax laws. It contains details that go far beyond the headlines, and those details are important to your financial well-being. The details associated with each new and amended rule are what will determine if money is going to come out of your pocket, or flow into it.

In order to understand and utilize the new tax law to your best advantage you need to go back to the current law and compare it with the latest changes. What's more, you need to know the effective date on various rules. Some are retroactive; some are prospective. It will be years before they are fully implemented. Sometimes it is vital to review the congressional tax-writing committees' thinking just to avoid unnecessary complications when planning and replanning your financial affairs.

That is the purpose of Part Two: The Specifics. Anyone can read newspapers, newsletters, and magazines. They will give you the once-over-lightly treatment. But to benefit from a true understanding of the law, you will have to dig much deeper. You can't afford not to.

Since it will be years before all the various provisions of this tax law will take full effect, you have the unique opportunity to profit from the tax changes during the period of transition. A missed opportunity cannot be reclaimed. So take the detailed information you get from Part Two: The Specifics, and apply it to the new tax planning opportunities available to you. You'll find a number of them explained in Part Three.

9

Details for individuals

The only way to appreciate the full impact of the 1986 Tax Reform Act on you, personally, is to take a set of 1986 income tax forms and figure your taxes under the new rules as if you were getting ready to file your 1987 return. You will keep all your salary and wages, dividends and interest, rents and royalties. Your capital gains will be figured differently; there will be no 60 percent exclusion available to you. You won't be able to income average or take the deduction for the two-earner couple. You get no dividend exclusion or sales tax deduction, and you may lose your IRA deduction, too. Medical expenses will probably be out since only amounts exceeding 7.5 percent of your income will be deductible. Unemployment compensation benefits will be taxed in full.

Obviously, there's still more. After all, this is a 1,000-page law.

After adjusting the forms to reflect your financial activities, you can apply the income tax rates that will be in effect when it's time for you to file by April 15, 1988. Then compare that tax liability with what you have for 1986. Then, and only then, can you truly make an observation about how, specifically, the 1986 Tax Reform Act affects you.

PERSONAL TAX RATES ARE SLASHED

Through 1986, single taxpayers must wade through fifteen tax brackets to compute their taxes. Married taxpayers filing jointly have fourteen brackets. Tax rates for both run as high as 50 percent.

When the House considered the idea of reducing tax rates, it came up with four rates: 15 percent, 25 percent, 35 percent, and 38 percent. The top rate would only apply to incomes over $100,000 for married couples and $60,000 for singles. The Senate wanted rates even lower, voting to utilize only two brackets of 15 percent and 27 percent.

Both plans are deceptively simple to understand and easy to handle. So, not surprisingly, the compromise has neither of these attributes.

Effective for 1987 (consider it a transitional year), there are five tax brackets ranging from 11 percent up to 38.5 percent. The top tax rate reaches married couples making over $90,000 and singles making more than $54,000.

In 1988, there are only two brackets—15 percent and 28 percent. The second tax bracket kicks in when income reaches $29,750 for married couples and $17,850 for singles. Then things get a bit complicated. Congress decided that it was unfair to let people making $250,000 a year pay tax at the same rate as those making $30,000. So they decided to phase out the benefits of the 15 percent bracket beginning in 1988, when a person's income became too high. Take, for example, a single taxpayer earning $75,000. Under the regular formula, she would pay 15 percent tax on the first $17,850, and 28 percent on the remainder of her taxable income. That's $2,677.50 plus $16,002, or $18,679.50. But once her income reaches $43,150, she starts to lose the tax benefit of the low, 15 percent tax bracket.

The way it's set up, married couples filing jointly begin losing the tax benefit when their income reaches $71,900. The phaseout is complete when their taxable income reaches $149,250. The range for single taxpayers is between $43,150 and 89,560. These amounts will be adjusted for inflation beginning in 1989.

THE STANDARD DEDUCTION REPLACES THE ZERO BRACKET AMOUNT

And it's about time. Taxpayers have been confused over the zero bracket amount since it was put into the law almost a decade ago. The standard deduction, on the other hand, has been like an old friend to taxpayers. They knew how it worked, and they were comfortable with it.

Well, now it's back. Here's how it's going to work.

For 1986, there is the old zero bracket amount. That means your itemized deductions will need to exceed $3,670 if you're married and filing jointly, $2,480 if you are a head of household, $2,480 if you are single, and $1,835 if you are married and filing separately before the next dollar is tax deductible. If you can't itemize the necessary expenses, then just go to the tax tables because the zero bracket amount is built into it.

For 1987, the standard deduction replaces the zero bracket amount. The levels are $3,760 for married couples filing jointly, $2,540 for heads of households and single taxpayers, and $1,880 for marrieds filing separately. You get this as a deduction whether or not you have enough expenses to reach this level. There is no floor for your total itemized deductions anymore.

For 1988, the numbers really go up. For marrieds filing jointly, the standard deduction is $5,000. For heads of household, it's $4,400; for singles, it's $3,000; and for marrieds filing separately, it's $2,500.

For 1989, the amounts from 1988 will be adjusted for inflation.

THE PERSONAL EXEMPTION TAKES ON NEW MEANING

Each personal exemption you claim on your tax return is worth $1,080 in 1986; $1,900 in 1987; $1,950 in 1988; and $2,000 in 1989. After that, the amount per dependent is adjusted for inflation. That's easy enough. Satisfy the five tests that qualify a person as a tax dependent, and you reap a windfall. The law does nothing to change those five requirements.

The elderly and blind lose their extra exemption, as of 1987. It's still available in 1986. However, as a bit of a bonus, Congress has agreed to increase the standard deduction by $600 for an elderly or blind individual, beginning in 1987. A single person who is either elderly or blind gets a $750 increase in the standard deduction, again beginning in 1987. What Congress gives with one hand, it takes away with the other.

The personal exemption seems pretty straightforward, but it's not—at least not for the high incomer. Just as the benefit of the 15 percent tax bracket is phased out for those with substantial incomes, so is the personal exemption. Beginning in 1988, married couples filing jointly with taxable income above $149,250 begin to lose the value of their personal exemptions. Single taxpayers begin to lose the value of their personal exemptions when income exceeds $89,560.

When it comes to your dependents, watch carefully what can happen to their taxes, and to yours. There's a new set of rules to learn. Effective after 1986, a person (probably a child) who is eligible to be claimed on another's tax return (usually a parent) will not be allowed to take the exemption on his or her return. For years, parents have been urging their children to work. Both would claim the dependency exemption, legally shielding a lot of income from tax. When the child has earned income (wages, salary, tips), the standard deduction can be used to offset it. So, a child will still be able to earn $2,540 in 1987 before any tax will kick in. What's more (and this gets a bit technical), a child's standard deduction is limited to the greater of $500 or his earned income, up to the standard deduction amount. So, the child can have at least $500 in unearned income and not pay any tax on it.

TWO TERRIFIC DEDUCTIONS ARE GONE—CASUALTIES OF TAX RATE CUTS

Congress has made the cut in tax rates the corner stone of tax reform. In order to pay the price, it found valuable tax breaks to repeal. Two that really hurt the working family are income averaging and the two-earner deduction.

Income averaging has been around for years. It's been modified and it's been amended time after time. But it has always worked. The purpose of income averaging has been to help ease the tax bite when you have a particularly good year after a couple of so-so years. Congress has explicitly stated that it no longer wants to offer that kind of tax relief after 1986. And that's a shame.

The repeal of the two-earner deduction hits particularly hard at households where husband and wife both work at paying jobs. The deduction is relatively new to taxes, being added to the law only a few years ago. The purpose was to try to ease the so-called marriage penalty. That's where two single people will pay substantially less tax than their married counterparts who hold similar-paying jobs. Take advantage of this deduction for one last time in 1986. It amounts to 10 percent of the smaller of the two salaries or $3,000, whichever amount is lower.

UNEMPLOYMENT COMPENSATION IS FULLY TAXABLE

Here's another short-sighted attempt by Congress to plug a perceived tax abuse. For years, unemployment compensation was completely tax-free. Then, Congress found that some well-to-do people were receiving benefits, and so it imposed a tax when income exceeded certain levels—$12,000 for singles, $18,000 for marrieds filing jointly. But after 1986, the exclusion from income is gone. All unemployment compensation benefits will be taxed. This will no longer be a loophole for tax abusers to wiggle through.

SCHOLARSHIPS AND FELLOWSHIPS ARE MUDDIED

The 1986 Tax Reform Act has muddied the waters when it comes to scholarship and fellowship grants, at least for the next few years. The way the law is written, there are now three distinct classifications of grants.

Scholarships and fellowships granted before August 17, 1986 will continue their tax treatment under earlier rules. If you have been receiving a tax-exempt grant, it retains that status. Good for you. Grants made after that but before 1987 will have split tax treatment. The amount received in 1986 will be taxed (or tax-free) under the old rules. Amounts received after 1986 will be taxed under the new rules.

Scholarships and fellowships granted in 1987 and later years are a different matter. Here, only grants made to cover tuition and course equipment will be tax-free. The wording is tricky. The amount of an otherwise-qualified scholarship received by a degree candidate is excluded from income up to the aggregate amount incurred by the student for tuition and course-related equipment during the period to which the grant applies.

And one more point. The amount of noncompensatory scholarship grants is considered earned income for purposes of figuring the dependency exemption.

AWARDS AND PRIZES ARE INCLUDED IN INCOME

There's no way around it. Scientific, achievement, and other awards and prizes are considered income. That's it. The only way to beat the system is to assign the prize to a tax-qualified organization. That way you don't have to report it as income, while at the same time you don't get a charitable contribution deduction.

Employee awards for safety and length of service are a different story. When the total value of awards to a single employee is under $1,600 a year ($400 when not under a qualified plan), then the employee pays no income tax, and the company still gets a legitimate business expense. Excess amounts are taxable, as are nonqualified gifts. Small-value items, such as pins, pens, company ties, and tote bags, are tax-free. So are traditional retirement gifts.

This loophole doesn't work for self-employed individuals. You can't give yourself a tax-free gift, have your sole proprietorship deduct it.

Awards and prizes that are free from income tax are also free from payroll taxes. Prizes subject to income tax are also subject to payroll taxes. That seems fair.

A NUMBER OF PERSONAL TAX BREAKS ARE REPEALED

Some taxes remain deductible; only one is repealed

Real estate taxes, state and local income taxes, and personal property taxes are all tax deductible to those who itemize their deductions in 1986 and future years. Even so, these deductions will be far less valuable in 1987 and later years simply because income tax rates are reduced.

Only the sales tax deduction bites the dust, beginning in 1987. And then only for individuals. Businesses and investors still get a break.

For individuals, it's no big deal. Sales tax has never been a particularly big deduction. It would have been far more serious if any of the other taxes had been repealed. As it is, taxpayers are lucky to have lost only this one. The biggest losers here are those who live in high sales tax states. Those who live in jurisdictions where there is little or no sales tax won't mind this tax law change.

Business owners and investors take note here. You can acquire property that would ordinarily be depreciated and when you do, the sales tax paid on the purchase will be added to the cost of the property for depreciation purposes. That's a sizeable tax break.

Charitable contributions are for itemizers only

This rule was not part of the Tax Reform Act. It has been on the books for some time now. Itemizers get to deduct 100 percent of their charitable donations in 1986. In 1987, they get nothing. Not a cent. To enjoy a charitable deduction in 1987 and later years, you will have to itemize your other deductions and, combined, they will have to exceed the increased standard deduction. All in all, only these taxpayers will be able to enjoy any tax benefit for their generosity.

Medical expenses are out for most

If you have a reasonably solid health care insurance plan, and if you are not struck down by a catastrophic illness or injury, then chances are you will not be able to deduct unreimbursed medical expenses beginning in 1987. That's because only medical expenses that exceed 7.5 percent of your adjusted gross income will be tax deductible. That's up from 5 percent in 1986. Remember the good old days when it was 3 percent?

There is an important exception that could help you get the deduction. The full cost of capital expenditures incurred to help a physically handicapped individual to reside in a personal residence is tax deductible as a medical expense. That includes such things as the construction costs of entrance ramps, widening doors, and the like.

Political contributions tax credit is repealed

With 1986 comes the last opportunity to make a political contribution and get credit for it on your tax return. You can claim a tax credit for half of your contribution, with a $50 limit for the credit for single taxpayers and $100 for married couples filing jointly. This is another one of those tax breaks that was repealed to accommodate the cut in tax rates. It was considered an unnecessary luxury by Congress. Still, they were not pleased that it had to go, since many small contributors relied on this credit. Without it, politicians may find their coffers a bit lighter at the time of the next election.

Military and clergy beat IRS

The military and the clergy have had a common enemy over the past few years—the IRS. It seems that the tax agency had declared war against both of these groups. They ruled that, effective July 1, 1983, clergymen and military personnel were illegally double-dipping when they received a tax-free housing allowance on the one hand, and then deducted their mortgage interest and real estate taxes on the other. The deduction for their interest and taxes would have to end, said the IRS.

Congress came riding to the rescue. Not only will the deductions stand, but they are good for past years, too.

This is one of those retroactive laws, only this one helps rather than hurts those taxpayers who are involved. If you think about it, how many wealthy ministers and military people have you seen lately flaunting the tax law?

Expenses for business and investment

Meal expenses. You better keep records of your business meals if you want your tax deduction to withstand IRS scrutiny. Business meals must be more than simply business-related. There must be the active conduct of business during, directly before, or directly following a meal for the price to be listed as a business expense. In addition, you must be able to verify who was entertained, when it took place, how much was spent, and the nature of the business relationship. Without such proof, you will be out of luck. Congress was explicit. The IRS is instructed not to accept estimates of business meal costs. Your only out is for a meal expense that is under $25. Anything over that and you must have an itemized receipt.

The 80-percent rule is straightforward. You have a business luncheon. Cost: $100, plus $18 tip, plus $5 tax. Total price: $123. Total deduction: $98.40. The 80-percent rule applies to the cost, plus tip, plus tax, beginning in 1987.

Lavish and extravagant meals are out. Only the price of regular meals is deductible. And the IRS will be the judge of what's extravagant and what's not. Ouch.

There are but a very few exceptions to this 80-percent rule. If you are reimbursed by your employer, you can deduct 100 percent of the cost of your business meals and include that reimbursement as income. It's your employer who is restricted to the 80 percent deduction. If you receive meals that are excluded from your income, there's no problem.

There's one interesting out that politicians will love. The cost of banquet meals is 100 percent deductible when the meal is part of the program, more than half of the participants are from out of town, there are at least 40 people attending, and the meal event includes a speaker.

Entertainment other than meals. When it comes to otherwise deductible entertainment expenses, only 80 percent will be deductible beginning in 1987. Again, there are a number of exceptions. If you are fully reimbursed by your employer, you have a wash. Your employer is subject to the 80-percent rule. The cost of traditional holiday business entertaining and similar events is fully deductible.

Travel expenses (other than to a convention). Someone got caught with their hand in the cookie jar. They decided to travel on business in the luxury of an ocean liner. So to stop that, Congress has limited the allowable deduction for luxury water travel to double the highest per diem rate paid for travel in the U.S. Of course, those attending a convention on a cruise ship are not subject to this limitation, but are still subject to the pre-existing limits on cruise ships.

The cost of educational travel is no longer deductible, as of 1987. Again, there were too many reported cases where teachers were bragging that they could tour the continent for the summer and write off the cost.

Charitable travel remains deductible, but only so long as there is no element of personal recreation and vacation involved.

Medical travel can still be listed as a medical expense, although it probably won't do you much good since the medical expense deduction will be unattainable for most people.

Regular business travel remains tax deductible. There was never any question about that.

Travel expenses (to conferences and conventions). The area of travel expenses has suffered a tremendous amount of abuse and Congress has been partially at fault for its exploitation. Many a congressman or senator was invited to speak (for a fee) at investment seminars and conventions at posh luxury resorts. Because of the new tax law, most of that is going to end.

The law provides that, as of January 1, 1987, only those costs of attending a convention or seminar that are directly related to your trade or business will be tax deductible.

No deduction will be allowed for travel or other costs of attending a convention, seminar, or similar meeting relating to investments, financial planning, or other income-producing activities. That includes registration fees, travel and transportation, meals, lodging, and whatever else you can think of to spend your money on. And that's that.

Fearful that someone would find a way to beat the new restrictions, Congress went one step further and said that a so-called business convention that does nothing more than pass out video tapes of proceedings will not be considered an active business convention, and expenses associated with it will not be deductible.

ITEMIZED DEDUCTIONS GET A NEW LOOK

Moving expenses

Beginning in 1987, work-related moving expenses will be deductible only as an itemized deduction, just like charitable contributions and mortgage interest. You will have to itemize to get any benefit and, of course, keep verifying receipts to back up your claim. In 1986, a person who has made a job-related move can deduct its cost whether or not he itemizes. The moving expense adjustment is being moved from a deduction from gross income to arrive at adjusted gross income, to a deduction from adjusted gross income to arrive at taxable income.

Unreimbursed employee business expenses and other miscellaneous expenses

These will be deductible only to the extent that, when added to your other miscellaneous itemized deductions, the total exceeds 2 percent of your adjusted gross income. So you will have to combine any unreimbursed employee business expenses with the cost of investment activities, union dues, tax preparation fees, and other tax-qualified miscellaneous itemized expenses. Compare that total with your adjusted gross income. Only amounts exceeding 2 percent will be tax deductible.

Effectively, that freezes most people out of claiming that deduction. For example, a person with a $45,000-a-year income needs $900 in these extra deductions before the next dollar is deductible. In the past, it was rare that a person could not claim at least a couple of hundred dollars a year in unreimbursed employee business expenses plus another couple hundred in miscellaneous expenses, especially something like job-hunting expenses. You could often combine a personal vacation with a job-hunting trip. Now it will be tough to garner any tax break for miscellaneous deductions because of the 2 percent limitation.

Consumer interest is hard hit

Aside from restrictions to Individual Retirement Accounts, the loss of the deduction for consumer interest will hit taxpayers the hardest. No longer will you be allowed to deduct what you pay to credit card companies on unpaid balances and cash advances. Interest charged on bank loans, car purchases, student loans, and any other type of consumer debt is subject to these new rules.

So that people wouldn't be thrown into shock, Congress decided to phase in the restriction on consumer interest deductions, beginning in 1987. For 1986, all of a person's consumer interest expense is tax deductible, assuming he itemizes his deductions on Schedule A.

In 1987, only 65 percent of that consumer interest will be deductible, 40 percent in 1988, 20 percent in 1989, and 10 percent in 1990. In 1991, not one thin dime of your consumer interest payments will be written off.

There are no exceptions.

The only way to beat this restriction is to pay for your purchases with cash drawn either from savings or from a home equity line of credit. Interest paid on home mortgages remains tax deductible.

Mortgage interest is still deductible

This remains one of the linchpins for individuals. You can continue to deduct the mortgage interest you have to pay to a lender covering not only your primary personal residence, but also that of a second or vacation home.

If you sell one property and replace it during the year, you can deduct the mortgage interest you pay on both. For example, say you have a retreat in the mountains, which you sell in October. In November, you purchase a beach cottage. The mortgage interest (and real estate taxes) on both are tax deductible. If you own one personal residence, sell it, and purchase a replacement during the year, you get to deduct all the mortgage interest paid on loans covering both homes. In addition, the closing costs that are otherwise tax deductible (such as interest and taxes), are deductible for both houses.

If you take out a line of credit, or refinance an existing mortgage, you will be entitled to deduct the interest you pay on the loans. They are considered mortgage loans and, as such, are tax deductible. The only restriction when it comes to refinancing is that you are not to refinance more than the original cost of the property (plus improvements) unless the extra money is going to be used for medical expenses, educational costs, or more home improvements.

Home ownership continues to generate terrific tax benefits. Two that have been available for years were not touched by tax overhaul.

If you sell one personal residence and replace it with a more expensive residence within two years either before or after the sale, you do not pay any income tax on your profit. Rather, the tax is deferred until you eventually sell for the final time. Your tax basis in the new property is reduced by the amount of your profit. Sorry, a loss on the sale of a personal residence is not deductible. It never has been, and probably never will be.

If you are past your 55th birthday when you sell your personal residence you can pocket, free of income tax, as much as $125,000 of your profit from the sale of the property. If you are married, your spouse must join you in electing this terrific tax treatment. It is a once-in-a-lifetime opportunity, so use it wisely. You will have to have lived in the residence three out of the past five years in order to qualify. The election is taken directly on the IRS Form 2119 for reporting the sale or exchange of a personal residence. The instructions to this form detail all the rules and regulations. They really are quite clear. Take advantage of this loophole because someday Congress may decide to close it.

Casualty losses are tightened a bit

Previously, individuals who suffered a casualty loss frequently would opt to skip making an insurance claim, preferring instead to pay the bill themselves in order to claim a tax break on their tax returns. After the first $100, casualty losses are deductible to the extent they exceed 10 percent of your income. Taxpayers would skip making an insurance claim because they feared that the insurer would cancel their policies. That's a real fear, but not one the IRS found persuasive. It fought this practice for years, arguing in court that in order to qualify for a casualty loss, a taxpayer first had to file a claim and see what the insurance company had to say. Now, Congress has made it law. If you don't contact your insurer, you cannot qualify for a casualty tax loss. Period.

Overseas workers receive a nasty surprise

At least some of them will. Effective in 1987, U.S. citizens living and working overseas who qualify for the annual exclusion of foreign-earned income will find that only the first $70,000 they earn is tax-exempt. In 1986, the exclusion is $80,000. This was scheduled to increase by $5,000 a year (beginning in 1988) until the exclusion finally reached $95,000. That's now only a memory. The limit is $70,000 a year.

Self-employeds get a break on their health insurance

It's not much, but something is better than nothing. Employees have long enjoyed health care coverage from their firms, paying no income tax on this fringe benefit. Also, all individuals, employee and self-employed alike, have been able to deduct medical bills they pay, once they meet the 5 percent (soon to be 7.5 percent) requirement to qualify for medical deductions.

At least for 1987 and 1988, self-employed individuals will be allowed to deduct 25 percent of the premiums they pay for health insurance coverage for themselves and their families. What's more, this is not an itemized deduction, but instead is a subtraction from gross income. You won't have to itemize in order to claim it.

Certain employee fringe benefits get a big boost

Group legal plans and educational assistance fringe benefits remain on the books at least another year. Through 1987, employees will be able to enjoy these fringes when they are offered through their employment. Whether Congress decides to extend them in the years ahead is anyone's guess. But they have been a part of the tax law for some time now, and there is a very good chance that they will be a part of it for years to come.

10

Details for investors

The 1986 Tax Reform Act has certainly received the attention from investors that it deserves. It has required them to sit up and take notice because to do otherwise would be financial suicide. That's putting the case in pretty strong but, nonetheless, accurate terms.

The reduction in overall income tax rates is welcomed by everyone. But look at the price investors will have to pay. Capital gains tax breaks are repealed. Depreciation on real estate has been substantially lengthened and otherwise made much less attractive than it once was. Rehabilitation of historic structures is much less of a tax incentive. The minimum tax has been strengthened and could cause substantial damage to the unwary. As an investment, real estate took some heavy hits. And even taking life insurance benefits on a monthly basis loses some of its appeal.

There are no two ways about it. The tax reduction expected from the cut in tax rates is carried on the backs of investors.

THE UNKINDEST CUT OF ALL: CAPITAL GAINS IS GONE

The repeal of the long-time tax break—capital gains—hits hard at all investors. Effective January 1, 1987, investors will no longer be allowed to exclude 60 percent of their profits from tax when they sell a security or other investment asset. All of it, 100 percent, will be taxed just like their regular income. That means salaries, wages, dividends, interest, and investment profits will all be lumped together into the same pot. There will be no more special preference given to investments.

Long-term capital gains has been part of the Internal Revenue Code in one form or another almost since its inception. So, to repeal this tax break is a radical departure from traditional tax overhaul. I suppose that's what makes this piece of tax legislation different from any other.

What the repeal means is that while income tax rates are dropping for individuals (first in 1987 and then again in 1988), they are doing just the opposite for investors. Rates will be lowest in 1986, substantially higher in 1987, and higher yet in 1988 and later years. Here's why.

Through 1986, investors will operate under the old law. The maximum income tax rate is 50 percent, and you will only pay tax on 40 percent of your net investment profits. That means the top capital gains tax rate is 20 percent. However, for many investors it is substantially less. Few people actually find themselves in the 50 percent tax bracket. A single person needs a taxable income of $88,270 to reach the 50 percent bracket; a taxable income of $50,000 results in a 42 percent bracket. A married couple filing jointly needs a taxable income of $175,250 to be in the 50 percent bracket; a taxable income of $50,000 means only a 38 percent tax bracket.

Take the example of a married couple in the 38 percent tax bracket, which is certainly more typical than someone in the 50 percent tax bracket. That couple's capital gains tax rate is a mere 15.2 percent (38 percent times 40 percent). Someone in the 42 percent tax bracket will pay a 16.8 percent capital gains rate. That's not too terribly onerous.

But beginning in 1987, investors will simply include their investment profits in their regular income, paying tax on it as if it were earned income from salary and wages.

The one exception is that for 1987 only, investment profits will not be taxed at any more than 28 percent. Nevertheless, that stands to be a hefty increase over 1986 rates, especially if your 1986 tax bracket is less than 50 percent.

In 1988 and later years, investment profits will be taxed just like regular income, without exception. If your taxable income is such that you lose the benefit of the 15 percent tax rate and the personal exemption, then so be it. Your investment profits could be taxed at rates as high as 33 percent.

There are a number of important details that bear mentioning. Watch these details carefully and you may benefit. Ignore them and you may unnecessarily overpay your taxes.

Installment reporting of securities transactions will not be allowed after 1986. If you sell profitable securities at the end of the year, you can decide which year you want to report your gain—1986 or 1987. If you can time your year-end selling program to take place between Christmas and New Years, you can juggle your income to your best advantage. Then, right after the first of the year, file for an automatic extention of time to mail in your 1986 return. That way, you will have until August 15, 1987 to decide which is the most advantageous year for you to declare your investment profits. Beginning in 1987, installment reporting of investment sales is prohibited.

Stock market activites are considered "active" rather than "passive" for investment purposes. When you consider the changes made to the tax law in the area of tax shelters and real estate investments, the distinction is important. Real estate and tax shelters are passive investments, and losses from passive investments are not deductible from salary and wage income, but can only be used to offset profits from passive investments. That doesn't include stock market activities.

Beginning in 1987, the distinction between long-term and short-term is unimportant. You will no longer need to look at your calendar when considering the ideal time to unload an investment. You will be buying and selling based on your investment ideas and instincts, rather than the dictates of the tax law. You will no longer need to hold on to an asset for more than six months prior to selling so you can qualify for long-term capital gains tax rates because there is no tax advantage to long-term capital gains.

One break that survived tax reform is that you still will pay no tax on a profitable investment while you still hold it. Your investments can appreciate, tax-deferred. Only when you sell will you have to report the transaction on your tax return.

Net profits from the sale of capital assets will be applied against net losses in determining whether you have a profit or loss on your investments for the year. Net profits will be fully taxed. Net losses will only be deductible up to $3,000 a year. Excess losses will be carried over to future years when they will be applied to profits for that year. Once again, any excess (up to $3,000) will be deductible.

Margin interest that you pay in cash management types of accounts will not be lumped together with personal consumer interest, but rather can offset investment profits.

DEPRECIATION IS CUT WAY BACK

Depreciation on real estate and other investments is much less attractive than it once was. Residential real estate placed in service after 1986 will have to be depreciated over 27.5 years on a straight line basis. That's 3.6 percent a year over 27.5 years, and that's not much of a deduction. Depreciation on commercial property is even worse. The depreciation deduction is taken over 31.5 years, again on a straight-line basis. That works out to a bit under 3.2 percent a year. Prior to this, real estate was depreciable over 15 years, or 18 years, or 19 years, depending when the real estate was first placed in service as an income-producing asset. What's more, the lion's share of the depreciation deduction was available to investors in the first years of ownership. No longer will real estate receive accelerated depreciation, and that's going to hurt real estate investors.

One important detail bears particular mention. Depreciable investment property that you have been claiming in years past will continue to carry the same tax treatment as under earlier rules. You don't have to switch midstream. The new rules only apply to property newly placed in service.

HISTORIC RESTORATION

The rehabilitation tax credit available to investors who work on historic properties is cut way back. The law through 1986 provides a 15 percent tax credit for nonresidential buildings at least 30 years old, a 20 percent credit for nonresidential buildings at least 40 years old, and a 25 percent credit for certified historic structures, including residential buildings. Under the new law, which affects property placed in service after 1986, there will be only two percentages—20 percent for rehabilitation expenditures on certified historic structures, and 10 percent on everything else that was placed in service before 1936. That represents a substantial reduction in the tax benefits that those involved in rehabilitation work had been counting on.

MINIMUM TAX TAKES SOME CAREFUL WATCHING

The minimum tax could become quite a problem if investors are not careful. The minimum tax has been around for some time now. It is a tax that is imposed on individuals who have otherwise found legitimate ways to reduce their tax burdens to next to nothing. Congress wants people to pay something toward the running of the government, even those individuals who have utilized the many tax preferences Congress has urged upon them. The solution has been the minimum tax. The problem with it is that almost no one has been trapped into paying it. The reason is that it's full of loopholes.

The basic structure of the minimum tax hasn't changed. Compute your income tax the regular way, and then compute the minimum tax. You pay whichever amount is largest. The tax rate (20 percent under old rules, 21 percent under new law) applies to a broader income base than that applied under regular income tax rules.

When you determine the income on which the minimum tax is based, you get a straight-away deduction. Married couples filing jointly can deduct $40,000. Singles deduct $30,000. Marrieds filing jointly deduct $20,000. That hasn't changed. However, there's one hitch. The exemption amount is reduced by $1 for each $4 your alternative minimum taxable income exceeds $150,000 (for marrieds), $112,500 (for singles), or $75,000 (for marrieds filing separately).

To determine your alternative minimum taxable income, add up all your wages, dividends, interest, investments, and other income, and add to that sum certain tax preferences you enjoy.

In 1986, the $100/$200 dividend exclusion was an item of tax preference. No longer, since that exclusion is repealed, effective January 1, 1987.

Accelerated depreciation on real property is an item of tax preference. So is some accelerated depreciation on personal property. Some expensing of intangible drilling costs will add to your tax base, as will tax breaks associated with certified pollution control facilities, the expensing of mining exploration and development costs, circulation expenses of magazines, newspapers, and the like, and research and experiment costs.

Net capital gains deductions (the 60 percent of an investment profit that remains untaxed) is an item of tax preference for 1986. After that, all investment income is fully taxed so it is automatically included in a person's calculations for minimum tax purposes.

Incentive stock options can increase your tax base. But the tax-exempt interest from municipal bonds does not. However, there is an exception here. Interest from private activity bonds may indeed be subject to the minimum tax. Find out from your broker if any bonds you hold, or are encouraged to purchase, may subject you to the minimum tax. The exempt portion of a U.S. citizen's income earned overseas while he lives and works abroad is not an item of tax preference.

Losses from passive investment activites can get you into minimum tax trouble. Through 1986, net losses from activities in which you do not materially participate, including passive farming activities, are not considered minimum tax preferences. But they are beginning in 1987.

Gifts of appreciated property to charitable organizations can increase your alternative minimum tax base. You get a full deduction for the fair market value of the gift. But the untaxed appreciated portion of the gift will be included in your income base.

Various itemized deductions are added back into income for purposes of computing your minimum taxable income. They include medical expenses (up to 10 percent of your income), miscellaneous itemized deductions, and state and local taxes, among others.

TAKE YOUR LIFE INSURANCE PROCEEDS AND RUN

Beneficiaries of life insurance policies who have taken installment payouts of life insurance proceeds have long enjoyed a double tax break. First, they have collected what amounts to the insurance portion of the payment tax-free. That's not going to change. Second, they have collected up to $1,000 a year in what amounts to interest on the balance in the account, tax-free, too. That annual $1,000 exclusion has just been repealed, effective for amounts paid with respect to deaths occurring after the 1986 Tax Reform Act was enacted. So, those who have been receiving payments all along will continue to enjoy that $1,000 exclusion. Only new beneficiaries will be fully taxed on the interest portion of the payments.

REAL ESTATE IS HARD HIT BY TAX REFORM

Real estate investors have been put into the same boat as other tax shelter investors. For all the details, see Chapter 11. It's important.

11

Details on tax shelters

It was the continuous, widespread, and highly publicized abuse of tax sheltered investments that caused the entire issue of tax overhaul to become such a national cause célèbre. Ordinary, everyday people felt they were being left out, even cheated, because they had to pay taxes and the superrich didn't. They were not able to take advantage of loopholes and preferences. Only those wealthy enough to afford tax losses were able to legally cheat the tax collector. That's what started the ground swell that eventually culminated in the Tax Reform Act of 1986.

So, Congress responded by putting an end to tax sheltered investments as we have come to know and appreciate them. Certainly there are still viable tax shelters available to investors. Your personal residence still throws off deductions for mortgage interest and real estate taxes. Interest from most municipal bonds remains tax-free. Interest on Series EE Savings Bonds can still be tax-deferred until they are cashed. Real estate investment trusts look good, and so do single premium whole life policies. IRAs and other retirement plans may or may not help as much as they have in the past. But these are not the shelters we've used so successfully and enthusiastically. Those are but a memory.

This much is certain. Tax shelters that forced you to pour money into a hole with no expectation of turning any sort of profit except for the tax savings no longer work.

TAX SHELTERS ARE DEFINED

Never before has there been a legal definition of the term "tax shelter." Prior to this law, the IRS and Treasury Department worked under the concept that an abusive tax shelter was one that cost the Treasury some money. In other words, the IRS had a free rein to go after whomever it pleased with no regard to what was a legitimate shelter and what was not.

That's all changed. A shelter is now legally defined as an investment where your deductions plus 300 percent of the tax credits associated with the investment result in no more than a $2 write-off for each $1 you invest in it. Stay within that two-to-one ratio and the IRS won't question you about the legitimacy of your investment. Get into something a bit steeper, and sooner or later the IRS will inquire.

A two-to-one write-off was the break-even point from a purely financial standpoint even before the law changed. You needed at least that. Anything better was pure gravy. Assuming you were in a 50 percent tax bracket, a $2 deduction resulted in a $1 tax benefit. You invested $1 out-of-pocket, never expecting to see it again. You got a $2 deduction for a $1 tax break. It's a wash. You could only hope that you might receive some sort of return on your investment over the years.

But with income tax rates reduced to no more than 38.5 percent in 1987 and 28 percent in 1988, a two-to-one write-off makes little sense unless you have high expectations of turning a profit somewhere down the line.

In addition, Congress has tightened up elsewhere in its effort to end abusive shelters.

THE INVESTMENT TAX CREDIT IS GONE

The businessman's and investor's favorite tax break was the Investment Tax Credit (ITC). It had been an important part of the tax code in one form or another since the early 1960s, except for a year or two when it was temporarily repealed. The ITC is what made many tax shelter deals work. The investor could take an immediate deduction against his tax liability for as much as 10 percent of the price of the investment. A tax shelter investor would purchase a $400,000 piece of equipment and immediately be eligible for a $40,000 reduction in his taxes. But he may have only put up a small portion of the purchase price out of his own pocket, financing the remainder.

Congress repealed the ITC retroactive to January 1, 1986. There's talk about reinstating it, but don't hold your breath. Congress will not be keen to resurrect the ITC, especially after the hard-fought battles that were necessary to get the 1986 Tax Reform Act through the House and Senate.

DEPRECIATION IS NOT NEARLY AS GENEROUS AS IT ONCE WAS

After the Investment Tax Credit, accelerated depreciation deductions were the tax shelter investor's best friend. Investors poured their money into deals where they enjoyed accelerated depreciation deductions that were entirely too generous. But they were part of the law as passed by Congress. People weren't doing anything the least bit shady. Rather, they were only taking full advantage of what Congress was encouraging them to do. They wanted people to put up buildings, apartments, drill for oil and gas, explore for minerals, and more. So people did, taking the depreciation deductions that Congress authorized.

But even Congress realized that a new piece of commercial real estate won't wear out over fifteen years, and it doesn't make sense to grant the largest portion of the deduction in the first few years you own the property. So, depreciation has been cut back in almost every case. However, keep this in mind. Any property that you have already placed in service and that you are already depreciating will continue on the depreciation schedule previously set for it. Only property newly placed in service is subject to the tougher depreciation standards.

When thinking of getting into an investment that involves depreciation, visit with a knowledgeable tax professional and run through the numbers before you invest. That's the only way to determine if the investment will work.

THE BIGGEST CHANGE IN TAX SHELTERS

You might think that repealing the ITC and scaling back accelerated depreciation deductions would be enough, but Congress took a final step. And that's the one that will spell the end for tax shelters. (Congress had to enact this new rule to take care of pre-existing shelters.)

No longer will tax shelter investors be permitted to deduct their tax shelter losses against otherwise regular taxable income. Technically, the law says limited partners are not actively engaged in running operations. They are only passive investors, and losses generated from a passive investment like a limited partnership will not be deductible against salary, wages, dividends, and interest, but may only be used to offset profits from similar passive investment activities.

That's important. Say you had been involved in a $3.50-to-$1 shelter. You invested $10,000 of your money, and in return you received $35,000 in tax deductions. Assuming a 50 percent tax bracket, your taxes were reduced by $17,500. You went out-of-pocket $10,000 and enjoyed a return of $17,500 for a $7,500 profit. That's pretty good, especially since you have losses rather than profits to report on your tax return.

But that only worked because you were allowed to apply that $17,500 against your other income. Now that you are not, you can sit with those losses forever and they won't do you any good.

Here's the important detail that you must keep in mind if you have previously been involved in limited-partnership tax shelter investments. There are two types of passive limited partnerships—those in which you invested prior to the date this tax legislation was enacted, and those in which you invested afterwards.

Losses from tax shelters purchased earlier will still be 100 percent tax deductible in 1986. Then in 1987, 65 percent of your losses will be deductible against salary and wage income. Those figures will fall to 40 percent in 1988, 20 percent in 1989, and 10 percent in 1990. Finally, any pre-existing tax shelter losses will not be deductible beginning in 1991. The nondeductible losses will have to be offset against tax shelter profits, carried over to future years, or recouped when the investment is sold.

Losses from tax shelters purchased after enactment are not eligible for a tax deduction in 1986 or any other year, for that matter, but may only be offset against profitable passive investments carried forward, or recouped.

Stock market gains and losses are considered to be the product of active pursuits, even when you turn over your entire portfolio to a broker or trust department to handle for you. No matter how passive you may be with your portfolio, stock investments are considered active and, as such, you get no offset against tax shelter losses.

REAL ESTATE

Real estate investing takes on a whole new meaning after tax reform. Perhaps most important, the law now defines it as a passive investment, just like a tax shelter investment. The general rule is that losses from real estate investments are not deductible against regular income, but rather must be offset against passive income, carried over to a future year if passive income is not available during the current year, or used to adjust the tax basis of the property when it is sold.

Also, real estate investors have been reduced to an equal footing with other investors. Congress has ordered that real estate investors limit their losses to amounts they have at risk in the enterprise. Investors in mining operations, oil and gas ventures, and other similar investments have been limited by at-risk rules for years. Only the real estate industry has enjoyed this special break. But it's gone, thanks to tax reform.

There is one important loophole available to the small real estate investor who likes to invest in homes, close to home. The law provides that if you actively manage your investment in, say, one, two, or even three townhouses, condos, or even separate-unit homes, you may qualify for special tax treatment. But you have to be active in your management of the properties. That means you must take an active role in approving tenants, setting rents, painting rooms, that sort of thing. If you just turn over the entire operation to a management firm, this preference won't be available to you.

Let's assume you are an active real estate investor. In that case, you should take all your rental income and subtract all your operating expenses, including depreciation. If there's a profit, report it.

But if there's a loss, you can deduct up to $25,000 worth so long as your income is less than $100,000 a year. If your income is over $150,000 a year, you get none of it. If your income falls in between, you qualify for a partial deduction only. You lose $1 of the deduction for each $2 your income exceeds $100,000. Any deduction you can't take is not lost, however. It can still be used in future years.

12

Details for tax-exempt bonds

Municipal bonds. Do they still make sense, or should you dump them? That's the question investors desperately want answered. It's simple enough. Compute your after-tax yield on a fully taxable corporate bond and compare it to the after-tax yield on a municipal. Choose the one that pays the highest yield and in so doing, keep risk to an acceptable minimum.

Understand that the equation on taxable versus non-taxable income has substantially shifted because of the latest tax law changes. Lower individual income tax rates have made tax-exempt income much less important, even less desireable than in years past. The tax-exemption has certainly lost quite a bit of its luster. Also, tax-exempt municipal bond interest will have to be reported to the IRS. Although most municipals remain tax-exempt, some bonds will throw off taxable interest income. It will pay you to know which are which. And even though some municipals remain tax-free, they may be subject to the toughened minimum tax. There's a lot to municipals these days, and it will be to your advantage to learn the details of the new rules. It could prove to be costly if you don't.

LOWER TAX RATES HURT TAX-EXEMPTS

The good news is that the interest on bonds issued by a state or local government to finance its official functions is still tax-free. Old bonds and new bonds, alike, are tax-free when used to further the government's needs.

When the income tax rates were as high as 70 percent, people would do almost anything to latch on to a solid tax-exempt municipal bond. Even when the maximum income tax rate was 50 percent, tax-exempt income looked pretty good. But with rates dropping to a low of 28 percent, you probably can do better with a fully-taxed investment than with a municipal bond—unless bond yields improve, that is.

You figure it out. Say a solid corporate bond is yielding 10 percent and municipals are paying 7 percent. If income tax rates are 70 percent on the corporate bond, then the after-tax yield would be only 3 percent. Not very good. If tax rates are 50 percent, the after-tax yield would still be only 5 percent on the corporate bond. The 7 percent municipal still beats it handily. But when tax rates drop to 28 percent, the yield on the corporate will be 7.2 percent. The municipal bond loses out after taxes are taken into consideration.

But personal tax rates don't drop to 28 percent until 1988. In 1987, the top rate is still 38.5 percent. You may be better off holding on to your municipals through 1987 when rates are still relatively high.

YOU WILL HAVE TO REPORT YOUR BOND INTEREST TO THE IRS

Beginning with your 1987 income tax return, you will have to fill in a special new line that asks how much municipal bond and other tax-exempt interest you received during the year.

In effect, some people do that now. Those claiming a sales tax deduction on Schedule A have to include in their adjusted gross income, other income that is not subject to tax. Examples are the untaxed portion of long-term capital gains, tax-free veterans' benefits, and, of course, tax-exempt interest from municipals. As you know, the sales tax deduction expires after 1986, so none of this applies to 1987 and future years.

Social security recipients must include on the front of their tax form 1040 (there's a parenthetical notation on line 21b) the amount of tax-exempt interest received during the year. It's needed to properly compute the amount of monthly social security benefits that will be subject to tax.

So you have to report your tax-exempt interest. So what? The IRS still isn't going to tax it. As yet there's no penalty to those who fail to report it properly, although Congress is likely to change that in the near future. And I don't expect Congress to impose even a minimal tax on municipal bond interest in the years ahead.

The reason why the IRS requires you to report your tax-exempt interest is so it can get a better idea of your economic income for audit selection purposes. Also, the IRS would like to know from some individuals where they got the money to purchase the bonds in the first place.

An integral part of the tax reform process has been to keep taxes in balance, neither raising nor reducing revenue. When a legislator had an idea that would reduce tax revenue, he had to come up with another idea to counter balance this loss. One device used to achieve balance was to give the IRS greater collection and administrative powers. Congress has told the IRS to get tougher with taxpayers, and it will. By knowing about an investor's tax-exempt income, the IRS can demand proof that the funds used to purchase the bonds were originally reported as taxable income.

Proof can be difficult if not impossible to produce in some cases. If a bond is newly purchased from new profits, you shouldn't have any problem. On the other hand, a bond that you've owned for years—some go out twenty years or more—could present a dilemma. Those records are hard to come by.

And what about a bond that you bought twenty years ago, swapped in a year-end tax deal, sold to invest in a mutual fund, and then later put back into another bond? Tracing that money over the past fifteen or twenty years could be an exercise in minutiae. But you'll have to do it if required by the IRS. Either that, or pay back taxes if the statute of limitations is still applicable, or stand the chance of being accused of tax fraud.

MOST BUT NOT ALL MUNICIPALS REMAIN TAX-EXEMPT

The new tax law sets out three types of municipal bonds. The most common type, the general bonds issued by a state or local government that are used to finance operations of the governmental unit, are tax free.

The second type is the private activity bond, the interest on which is taxable.

And finally, there's the private activity bond that has a special exemption from taxation written into the tax law. They include exempt-facility bonds used to finance airports, docks, wharves, water and sewage facilities, and the like. There are also special exemptions for qualified mortgage and veterans' mortgage bonds, small-issue bonds, student loans bonds, and bonds issued by tax-qualified charitable and educational organizations.

When it comes to private activity bonds, the key date is September 1, 1986. The new definitions and tax rules apply to those issued on or after September 1, 1986.

Another key is that taxable private activity bonds will carry a higher rate of return than their tax-exempt cousins. If your tax bracket is low, the greater return may make the taxable bonds a preferable investment.

THE MINIMUM TAX BEARS WATCHING

Tax-exempt interest from general municipal bonds never has been and never will be considered an item of tax preference, even though there was some talk about making that the case. That means you do not have to add the interest you collect from tax-exempts to your tax base for purposes of calculating the minimum tax.

Interest collected from taxable private activity bonds is already included in your income, so for minimum tax purposes, it doesn't make any difference whatsoever.

However, tax-exempt interest paid on private activity bonds (remember, they have a special exemption written into the law) will be considered a tax preference item beginning in 1987. You will have to include this interest as part of your income subject to the minimum tax. With that rate jumping to 21 percent in 1987, it's a stiff price to pay on otherwise tax-free income. So consider the minimum tax consequences when investing in private activity bonds.

13

Details on retirement planning

The rules as we know them have just been overhauled. You have to relearn almost everything you ever learned about IRA's, corporate plans, SEP-IRAs, vesting rules, and more.

And it is important that you do. Social security will be around when you decide to quit work. And chances are that your company pension will send out checks every month. But those two items won't be enough. You will need to supplement them with income from your own savings and retirement plans. And you need to get the most out of each retirement dollar you can set aside.

After all, remember the purpose of retirement planning. You want safe, financially secure years once you leave the workforce. You will not want to have to watch every nickel, but will much prefer to overindulge your grandchild. You have that choice. All you have to do is learn the new details of retirement planning so you can watch your nest egg grow as rapidly as it should.

The biggest thing that happened to retirement planning is that, beginning in 1987, IRAs are restricted for about 25 percent of the people who have these accounts. Those with deferred compensation plans will not be able to salt away nearly as much as they have over the past couple of years. More people than ever will qualify for pensions through their employment thanks to a tax law change, but those who receive lump-sum distributions when they leave an employer will be more heavily taxed on their money than in the past. Government workers must learn to live with a new pension rule that immediately taxes their monthly checks.

INDIVIDUAL RETIREMENT ACCOUNTS ARE NOT FOR EVERYONE

At least not anymore. Early on, when Congress first decided that it was a good idea for people to start planning for their own retirement needs, they set up a plan under which only those individuals who were not covered by a company retirement plan could have their own Individual Retirement Accounts. That seemed fair. Those workers who were not covered by a plan needed to provide for themselves, and a tax break would encourage them to do so. Those workers who were covered by a plan shouldn't be entitled a tax deduction.

Then the nation's banks got into trouble. Money flowed out of banks and savings and loans, and was placed into money markets and other mutual funds in record amounts because these were paying higher interest rates than were the financial institutions. Consequently, the idea evolved to open up IRAs to every worker, since most would put their funds into the banks.

That proved to be true. Workers flocked to their local financial institutions to plunk down their $2,000 (it once was $1,500), knowing that the contribution to their retirement account was tax deductible, and that any dividends and interest would accumulate on a tax-deferred basis.

At last count, more than 24 million individuals had invested in IRAs. The money these accounts represent, when combined with the amount in Keogh plans (for the self-employed), has produced the more than $270 billion invested in individual retirement plans. More than half of it lies in financial institutions. Bankers love IRA money; it's what they consider long-term money—money that will be on deposit for twenty or thirty years, or more. It's money that can be lent to others to make money for the bank.

Of the 24 million IRA owners, just one out of four will be affected by the changes made to the tax law under the 1986 Tax Reform Act. Three out of four will operate under the rules in effect prior to the new law.

You will still be able to contribute as much as $2,000 a year, or 100 percent of your income, whichever is less, and deduct your contribution on your tax return. Spousal IRAs, (that's where only one spouse works) are limited to $2,250 divided between the husband's and the wife's accounts. No more than $2,000 can be put into one, no less than $250 into the other. If both husband and wife work, they can each contribute $2,000 for a combined family contribution and deduction of $4,000. All this is available to everyone through the end of 1986 because the new tax law does not begin to affect taxpayers until 1987.

Actually, that's not entirely true. Individuals have until the due date of their returns, without extensions, to make their tax deductible contributions to their IRAs for 1986. That means you have until April 15, 1987 to make your 1986 IRA contribution. (For the self-employed individual who is making a Keogh plan contribution, you have until August 15, 1987 to make your contribution, as long as your plan is set up by year-end. Just make certain that you have applied for an automatic four-month extension of time to file your return.)

When the new law kicks in, you have only to determine your particular status to see precisely how the tax changes will affect your tax situation. These are the possibilities:

1. If you are single and not covered by a company retirement plan, you can contribute to an IRA and deduct your contribution.

2. If you are single and are covered by a company retirement plan, and your income is under $25,000 (before considering an IRA contribution and deduction), you can still deduct the amount of your IRA contribution, up to the legal limit.

3. If you are single and are covered by a company retirement plan, and your income is between $25,000 and

$35,000, you can deduct only a portion of your IRA contribution. For each $5 your income is above $25,000, you lose $1 worth of your IRA deduction.

4. If you are single and are covered by a company retirement plan, and your income is over $35,000, you cannot deduct any portion of your IRA contribution.

If you are married and either one of you is covered by a company retirement plan, then the other is considered to be covered by a company plan as well for purposes of determining your eligibility for the IRA deduction.

5. If you are married and neither of you is covered by a company retirement plan, you can deduct your IRA contribution. That might include a contribution for yourself, for the two of you if both work, or a spousal IRA if only one works.

6. If you are married and either one of you is covered by a company plan, then you can still deduct your IRA contributions when your income is under $40,000.

7. If you are married and either one of you is covered by a company plan, then you can deduct a portion of your IRA contributions when your income is between $40,000 and $50,000 a year. The amount of the IRA deduction is reduced by $1 for each $5 your income exceeds $40,000.

8. If you are married and either one of you is covered by a company plan, then you cannot deduct one red cent for your IRA contribution when your income exceeds $50,000.

That's pretty straightforward.

However, the law goes on to encourage people to make what's known as a nondeductible IRA contribution. The carrot is that the dividends and interest earned in the account over the years is tax-deferred. The stick is that you tie your money up for the long haul. If you have to tap into it, you will be roundly taxed and penalized.

The big winners here are those people who salted away money over the years in their IRAs. When they contributed $2,000 to an account and their tax bracket was 42 percent, they received a $840 tax benefit. The interest will continue to grow tax-deferred, and they will tap into it in retirement, probably at a 28 percent tax rate. So if you're one of these lucky individuals you can take out $2,000 once you've passed age 59 and one-half, and you'll pay a tax of only $560. Your tax profit will be $280.

Multiply that by thousands of dollars and you can see what an attractive investment this has been.

But now you can no longer make the claim that when you retire you will probably be in a lower tax bracket than people are today. You won't be. There's only one high tax bracket, and that's 28 percent. If you are eligible for an IRA, your tax benefit is 28 cents on the dollar. If you withdraw from an IRA, your tax is 28 cents on the dollar. Your only tax benefits are that you get a current tax deferral, which may or may not be a true tax advantage. And the money in your account accumulates tax-free until withdrawn.

The law allows—no, change that to encourages—people to make nondeductible contributions to their retirement accounts. It's not a smart idea. The details just don't work out. You will be tying up your money in a long-term investment that you can't get into without paying tax as well as a substantial (10 percent) penalty. If you've been contemplating making a nondeductible contribution to an IRA in 1987 or later, think twice about it. You might prefer to invest in something that you can get into without paying such a stiff penalty. After all, you no longer get to deduct your contribution, so what's the real point? The shine has truly been taken off the Individual Retirement Account.

Some people had thought they had a good plan to utilize the nondeductible IRA contribution. They thought that all they had to do was establish a separate IRA funded with nondeductible contributions, and keep it apart from the IRA they had established with tax-deductible contributions. Then if you had an emergency and had to get some money, you could make a withdrawal from the nondeductible IRA account. You would already have paid tax on it, so you wouldn't be taxed twice. You would have to pay a penalty, but what the heck. You need the money. But Congress took care of that idea before it had a chance to catch hold by ruling that if you had, say, an $8,000 IRA funded with tax-deductible contributions and a $2,000 IRA funded with nondeductible contributions, and you wanted to withdraw $1,000, the IRS would consider $800 to come from the first account, and only $200 from the other. You would be taxed on the $800 withdrawal, but not the $200 (as long as it represents principal, and not interest). The penalty would apply, too.

If you can still make an IRA contribution and deduct it (or at least most of it), make the contribution. You will be glad you did once retirement years start to roll around. But if the contribution is not deductible, you will probably be better off investing elsewhere.

U.S. GOLD AND SILVER COINS ARE FINE FOR IRAs

Congress wants you to buy U.S. gold and silver coins, and if they can entice you to put your IRA money into them, so much the better. Chances are you won't be selling any time soon. So, to encourage sales, Congress released the ban it had once placed on putting IRA assets into these coins. However, Congress went no further. You cannot use any other type of collectible for your IRA. That means you cannot invest in oriental rugs, stamps, lithographs, or anything of a similar nature for your IRAs. The only place for your money is in a mutual fund, certificate of deposit, stocks and bonds, or a bank account.

WHERE YOU STICK YOUR IRA IS IMPORTANT, TOO

With the capital gains tax break repealed as of Janaury 1, 1987, you may want to rethink your investment strategy for IRAs. If you've shied away from investments because dividends and interest were yielding more money, take a second look once the new tax law takes effect. Growth stocks may increase their yields to be competitive with other investments.

POPULAR DEFERRED COMPENSATION PLANS WILL STILL BE THE RAGE

While you will no longer be allowed to contribute more than $7,000 of your own money into a 401(k) deferred compensation plan, you will still receive excellent benefits. What's more, you have through the end of 1986 to make as large a contribution to your plan as you can afford. If you can, defer income in 1986 when rates are high, until 1988 when rates will be lowest.

With deferred compensation plans, you will be able to make hardship withdrawals up to the amount you contributed to the plan although you will be taxed and penalized. You may need money to pay emergency medical bills, or to put toward higher education. Those are two reasons that have always been acceptable to the IRS.

Deferred compensation plans are still terrific despite the $7,000 limitation. Only the very top income bracket people ever deferred more than that. It's a darn sight better than the measly $2,000 available to people who have IRAs.

SEP-IRAs SHOULD BECOME POPULAR AS MORE EMPLOYERS INSTALL THEM

SEP-IRA is nothing more than an Individual Retirement Account (IRA) plan that's run through your employer. SEP stands for Simplified Employee Program. The firm gets together with the employees; each individual has set up his or her own personal IRA. The firm then makes contributions directly to each employee's IRA. The employee doesn't pay any payroll taxes on his or her contribution, which is an important tax savings.

VESTING RIGHTS START EARLIER

Traditionally, firms set employee vesting rights as far into the future as possible. In the past, it wasn't unusual to find firms requiring 10 years of full employment before an employee could be entitled to any retirement benefit. The idea was that many employees would leave a firm well before their pension rights became vested. The ex-worker would get nothing. The money that was accumulating in his or her account would then either go back into the general treasury or would be used to supplement and increase everyone else's pensions.

Under the new law, an employee must be fully vested (entitled to pension benefits) after five full years on the job. Or, if the employer doesn't want to use a five-year vesting period, he must start providing vested rights of 20 percent after only three years, adding 20 percent each year until the employee is fully vested after seven years.

Keep this detail in mind as you consider job moves. One more week in a place might be worth thousands when you turn 65.

When you do retire, no one is going to come looking for you to pay you your pension. You will have to apply to every firm you worked for over the years to claim your pensions. Because of the 1986 Tax Reform Act, you could be entitled to lots of them.

14

Details on family and estate planning

Once again, a lower tax rate indicates that a rethinking of family and estate tax planning is necessary. With the IRS taking no more than 28 cents on the dollar, you don't need to shift quite as much money over to a child in a tax-saving effort. What's more, many long-time tax saving devices are no longer available. Clifford trusts and spousal remainder trusts no longer work as intended. Trusts and estates will be subject to the same tax rates as individuals, and will have to pay quarterly estimated taxes. Children under the age of 14 will be taxed on unearned income at their parent's highest marginal tax rate when they try the old income-shifting strategies. What's more, children will lose their personal exemptions when they are eligible to be taken as a dependent on a parent's return. All these new rules will make but a fond memory the possibility of income shifting in order to save on taxes. Here are the details of what will be necessary in handling an estate or trust, or in trying to shift income between family members.

ESTATE AND TRUSTS USE A NEW TAX RATE SCHEDULE

Beginning in 1987, the income tax schedule for estates and trusts is:

If taxable income is	The tax is
$ 500 or below	11% of taxable income
$ 500 to $4,700	$55 plus 15% if the excess over $500

$4,700 to $7,550	$685 plus 28% of the excess over $4,700
$7,550 to $15,150	$1,483 plus 35% of the excess over $7,550
Over $15,150	$4,143 plus 38.5% of the excess over $15,150

For 1988, the tax rate is more simple—15 percent on the first $5,000 of taxable income in the estate or trust, and 28 percent on the excess. However, that 15 percent tax bracket is phased out quickly. The phaseout begins once taxable income reaches $13,000 and is completely phased out once it reaches $26,000.

Estates had been able, in the past, to use a special rule that allowed them to be taxed under the same rates as a married person filing separately. No longer. Now estates and trusts are taxed alike on earned income.

TRUSTS AND ESTATES MUST PAY QUARTERLY ESTIMATED TAXES

It's a burden. No question about that. Estates and trusts will have to settle up their income tax accounts with the IRS each quarter, or pay the underpayment-of-estimated-tax penalty. Under earlier law, there was no estimated tax payment requirement. To ensure that estates which will go out of business in a relatively short period of time won't be overly burdened, the law provides that estates not be required to make quarterly payments within the first two years of existence.

And there's an important out for trusts, too. The trustee making estimated tax payments can, in effect, give the beneficiary credit for the tax payments of the trust. The election must be made within sixty-five days after the end of the trust's tax year.

NEW TRUSTS MUST USE THE CALENDAR YEAR

Under old law, a trust using a fiscal year other than a calendar year was able to manipulate income and deductions to the best interests of the trust beneficiaries. No longer. Most newly-created trusts now have to adopt the calendar year as their own.

CLIFFORD AND SPOUSAL REMAINDER TRUSTS ARE OUT

For years, high-income individuals with income-producing assets could transfer those assets to their children using either a Clifford trust or a spousal remainder trust. With a Clifford trust, the income generated from the trust assets went to the low-tax-bracket children. At a predetermined period (which had to be more than ten years), the trust assets reverted to the donor-parents. It was a wonderful technique for lending assets to a child, while not letting him really get his hands on them. The child could grow up and, hopefully, use the lightly-taxed money for college tuition, room, board, or to purchase a house or finance a business.

The spousal remainder trust worked just like a Clifford trust with two important exceptions. This trust did not have to last any predetermined period: further, when it was dissolved, the assets reverted not to the donor-parent, but to the donor's spouse. Hence, the name: spousal remainder trust.

Clifford trusts and spousal remainder trusts set up prior to March 2, 1986 will keep their tax-preferred treatment so long as no additional transfers to it are made. The income will be taxed to the children. Income from newer trusts will be taxed to the donors.

INCOME SHIFTING BECOMES SUPERFLUOUS

Why worry about shifting income to a child or other lightly-taxed family member when everyone is going to be paying the same rate of tax? If your maximum tax rate is 28 percent (which it will be for 1988), and you transfer income-producing assets to a child whose tax rate will also be 28 percent, you've saved nothing. Even if the child's rate is a low 15 percent, the tax savings may not be significant, especially on smaller amounts of money.

What's more, increasing a child's income for a tax advantage loses some of its appeal now that the family cannot claim a double personal exemption for the child. Under the old law in effect through 1986, the parent and the child were both allowed personal exemptions for the child, assuming the parent supplied at least half of the child's support. The new rule says that if a child can be taken as a dependent on a parent's return, then the child can't take advantage of his or her own personal exemption. That's worth $1,900 in 1987, and more later on.

Perhaps more important is the new rule that taxes a child's income at the parent's highest marginal tax bracket on income from assets transferred to the child. Go ahead and give little Jenny $20,000. You and your spouse can do that without running afoul of the IRS's gift tax rules. But at 8 percent interest, that comes to $1,600. Since her income exceeds $1,000, she will be taxed at her parent's highest tax rate. There is one important out. Jenny gets the first $1,000 she collects in unearned income at her own tax rate. Unearned income is dividends, interest, rents, royalties, profits from securities transactions, that sort of thing. Earned income, on the other hand, is from wages and salary. A child can earn thousands before eating up the entire standard deduction. As a result, a working child will pay much less tax than a child collecting passive income.

As usual, when there is a rule, there is an exception. Children age 14 or older are not going to be taxed at the parents' high marginal tax rate on income from assets given by their parents. So, parents have at least the high school years to think about transferring income-producing assets to their children for the four years prior to high school and even beyond while they attend college. But don't do it earlier. There's just no tax benefit to it.

15

Details on new business rules

You're going to hear a great deal of talk over the next few years about the enormous impact of the 1986 Tax Reform Act on business. You'll hear that "C" corporations (those are regular corporations) will be phased out of existence where possible, especially those owned by individuals. The reason is that corporations will no longer provide the wonderful tax shelter that they once did. You'll hear how subchapter S corporations (those are hybrid organizations) are incorporated on the one hand, but taxed much like a partnership on the other.

Yet, when all is said and done, the fact remains that the small business is the single best tax shelter available in the tax code today. You can't do better than work for yourself and enjoy each and every tax break still available to you. And there are hundreds. All you have to do is beware of the new pitfalls written into law by the Tax Reform Act, and take legal advantage of the remaining tax preferences available to you and your business.

CORPORATE RATES ARE CUT FOR BIG BUSINESS, BUT NOT FOR SMALL; CORPORATE CAPITAL GAINS RATES ARE BOOSTED

You've undoubtedly heard that business will benefit from tax reform because of the substantial cut in corporate income tax rates. Well, that's true, but only as far as it goes. What they fail to tell you is that big business wins, and small business gets nothing. As of July 1, 1987, the top corporate income tax rate is dropped to 34 percent. But that's the top rate. Most small business pays nothing close to that rate.

Up until that time, the current tax rate schedule remains in effect.

Taxable Income	Tax Rate Percentage
$25,000 or less	15 percent
$25,000 to $50,000	18 percent
$50,000 to $75,000	30 pecent
$75,000 to $100,000	40 percent
Over $100,000	46 percent

Unless a corporation's taxable income is above $75,000 prior to the tax revision, the cut in corporate tax rates won't help curb the tax bite.

When it comes to corporate capital gains, however, the tax rate is raised to conform to the regular 34 percent rate for corporate taxable income. That's up from 1986's 28 percent. Individual capital gains rates increase from 20 percent in 1986, to 28 percent in 1987, to a possible 33 percent in 1988. Corporations experience a much smaller increase from 28 percent in 1986 to 34 percent in 1987.

STILL NO DEDUCTION FOR DIVIDENDS PAID OUT

One argument against the corporate form of doing business is that the corporation has two masters to please-- the shareholders and the IRS. The shareholders want their dividends, and the IRS wants the shareholders to get them. That's because corporations cannot deduct the dividends they pay out. In effect, the IRS gets paid twice, first by the corporation on profits that are paid to shareholders as dividends, and then again when the shareholder declares his dividend income.

There has been talk for years about allowing corporations at least a partial deduction for the dividends they pay. But it has never come to pass. Corporate profits are still double taxed.

THE DIVIDENDS RECEIVED DEDUCTION IS CUT, TOO

Corporations have long been allowed to invest in other corporations. And when they do, they receive dividends just like any other shareholder. For years, corporations have been allowed to exclude 85 percent of the dividends they have received from their investments in other businesses. As part of the move to generate a bit more revenue, Congress decided to cut back on this preference. Beginning in 1987, the dividends received deduction is scaled back to 80 percent.

BUSINESS MEALS AND ENTERTAINMENT EXPENSES ARE ONLY 80 PERCENT DEDUCTIBLE

President Carter screamed about the three-martini lunch. Others have watched in horror or envy as expense account travelers have run up huge tabs. You can't go to a hotel without seeing business conventions, seminars, and meetings taking up all the available space. Business moves America, and business is certainly what makes the hotel and food business the enterprise it is today.

But Congress feels that too much of a tax break has been given for business travel and entertainment. So, it has decided to cut it back, effective Janaury 1, 1987, to 80 percent of what is spent on meals and entertainment. What's more, Congress has instructed the IRS to be a stickler for records and receipts on these expenses, ordering the agency to demand proof that the expense was incurred while the taxpayer was directly engaged in business (before, during, or after the meal or entertainment). Without proof that the event was directly related to business, rather than simply conducive to a business discussion, you won't be allowed to claim your expenses on your tax return. Why does Congress want the IRS to crack down even harder here than in years past? To collect more revenue, that's why.

WHY SMALL BUSINESS IS STILL THE BEST PLAY IN TOWN

You can still deduct the cost of owning and operating a business. Fees for accounting advice, legal services, wages, salaries, tax payments, utilities, and more are all tax deductible, just as they have been.

No other group can make the same claim. Investors are hurt terribly by the loss of capital gains. Those saving toward retirement are hurt by tougher requirements for IRAs, deferred compensation plans, and more. Individuals are hurt by the loss of the deductions for consumer interest, restrictions on miscellaneous deductions, sales taxes, medical expenses, and charitable contributions, among others.

But small businesses still have it all, or at least most of what they had prior to tax overhaul. You can still attend conventions that are directly associated with your trade or business and deduct the cost. Travel costs, registration fees, rooms, taxis, 80 percent of meals, and other expenses are deductible. However, similar expenses put out to attend an investment or educational seminar are no longer deductible, as of January 1, 1987.

THE 10 PERCENT INVESTMENT TAX CREDIT IS REPEALED

This extremely valuable tax credit was repealed, effective January 1, 1986. No, that's not a misprint. It was repealed retroactively. But it came as no surprise. Throughout the evolution of this tax law, Congress promised to strike this tax break. And they did. You can no longer reduce your taxes by 10 percent of the price of the new equipment you buy during the year, or 6 percent of the cost of a new car. Even when Congress limited the amount of investment tax credit you could claim in any one year, especially on car purchases, it was still a most valuable tax preference. Too bad it's gone.

But Congress added something in its place that helps the small business operator. And that's the amount you can expense in one year. Following are the particulars.

EXPENSING ALLOWANCE HAS BEEN DOUBLED

Depreciation can be a pain to figure and keep track of. So, a few years back, Congress decided that it no longer required businesses to depreciate wastebaskets, typewriters, and other items. Up to $5,000 worth of depreciable property was allowed to be written off—all at once—in any one year. That was great. You didn't have to keep those detailed records years after year. And now, thanks to tax reform, you can write off the first $10,000 worth of business property you purchase during the year. This $10,000 allowance starts to be phased out when you purchase more than $200,000 worth of tangible personal property in any one year. But that's OK. You can plan your purchasing in such a way as to take full advantage of the opportunities that present themselves for expensing business assets.

DEPRECIATION RULES TAKE ANOTHER HIT

There's only one good thing that Congress has done about the depreciation in the last decade and that is, it has ended any debate between the IRS and taxpayers about the useful life of any asset. Now, by law, there are specific classifications of property. You can't argue that it has a shorter life span, and the IRS can't argue that it has a longer one. Useful life was always a bone of contention because it seemed that no matter what you claimed was an asset's useful life, the IRS would say it was longer, and it was up to you to prove that the IRS was wrong. A difficult proposition. Now, useful life is an audit-proof issue.

So much for the good Congress has done. The bad news is that Congress has upset the applecart yet one more time. It set out a new accelerated depreciation system in 1980, replacing the existing system. It changed it two more times between 1981 and 1986, at which time it passed the 1986 Tax Reform Act. At this point, depreciation is such a hodgepodge that it is almost impossible to decipher.

Keep this important detail in mind. Any property that has been the subject of depreciation in the past will continue to get the same depreciation treatment in the future until it is either fully depreciated or disposed of. If you have been depreciating your business real estate over 6 years under an accelerated plan, go right ahead and enjoy that depreciation deduction method for the remaining 9 years or so. If you buy commerical real estate now, you will have to employ a useful life of 31.5 years, and use a straight-line depreciation method. Just go by the rules in effect at the time the property was purchased and placed in service.

LUXURY CARS ARE STILL A BIG ISSUE

Congress finally got around to closing off an abusive tax shelter that less well-to-do individuals found difficult to accept. Doctors, lawyers, corporate execs, and others were buying big, fancy cars and writing off thousands of dollars every year on them. A business person would buy a $50,000 car and let the business pay for it. The employee could only afford a Chevy.

To put an end to some of the abuse, Congress restricted the amount of investment tax credit that could be taken on a new car. (Of course, that's beside the point now that the ITC has been repealed.) In addition, Congress voted to limit the amount of depreciation that could be taken on any car in any one year. It is not nearly as high as it once was. To see exactly what those limits are, see chapter 7.

THE CORPORATE MINIMUM TAX GETS TOUGHER

Detail is important here when talking about the corporate minimum tax. Corporations will have to pay a heftier corporate minimum tax if it amounts to more tax than what is computed under the regular tax system. Similar to the individual income tax, the corporate minimum tax is based on the corporation's minimum taxable income. That's its regular taxable income plus a number of tax preferences that ordinarily escape taxation.

The tax rate was just boosted by five percentage points to 20 percent by the Tax Reform Act.

There is an exemption amount—$40,000, but it is reduced by $1 for each $4 the corporation's income exceeds $150,000.

A TOUGH NEW ACCOUNTING RULE FOR SMALL BUSINESS

You have to adopt the calendar year as your tax year unless you can come up with a compelling reason for the IRS to let you use another tax year. Sometime in 1987, most partnerships, subchapter S Corporations, and personal service corporations will have to adopt the calendar year. That's an expensive proposition from a tax standpoint. For years, savvy business operators have used a different tax year for their business year, so they could manipulate income and deductions to their best advantage between themselves, personally, and their businesses. They could use their firms as their own private banks for at least a year at a time. They could declare bonuses so the tax wouldn't be due for a year to 18 months. They could keep income in a business where it would be lightly taxed and paid out the next year when it was more advantageous. That's over. And that's a shame.

16

Details on new compliance rules

Congress wants the IRS to collect more taxes from people who make mistakes on their returns, who don't pay enough quarterly estimated taxes, and who fail to send all the information reports that are required by law. In short, it wants to penalize anyone and everyone who doesn't toe the line. Congress feels it is easier to get tougher with existing taxes than it is to impose new taxes.

It's an easy technique for Congress to adopt. New penalties have been added that will bring in millions of dollars. It decided that the government pays too much interest to taxpayers who are owed money on overpayments, so it set up a different interest rate for them. The IRS will receive more reports on people's financial dealings so they can't slide through any crack in reporting their sales and exchanges. Here are some of the details, and why they were finally made part of the law.

THE IRS PAYS LESS INTEREST, COLLECTS MORE

If you owe the IRS, you have to pay interest. If the IRS owes you (and doesn't pay promptly) it has to pay interest to you. It was always been the same interest rate up until now, that is. Now the rate that the IRS charges will be one percentage point higher than the rate it has to pay out. That's not fair, but that's the new rule. Sorry. And so they can adapt more quickly to fluctuations in market interest rates, the IRS will set them quarterly, using comparable interest rates on Treasury securities as a guide.

BIG BROTHER IS WATCHING

No question about it. The IRS wants to know all. And Congress has just about given the tax agency free rein. Beginning in 1987, real estate transactions will be reported to the IRS, usually by the settlement attorney. The IRS wants to make certain that you report the sale or exchange of your personal residence. This is especially important now that the capital gains tax break has been repealed.

If you have a government contract, the federal agency will inform the IRS that you work for it, the amount you are paid, and other pertinent identifying information. Again, they want to make sure that you report all the income you're required to report. This, too, begins in 1987.

Royalty payments will have to be reported. That can be tricky, so watch carefully here. When you receive a 1099 income information slip showing the royalty income and how it was reported to the IRS, make sure you either report it the same way on your return, or attach a note to your return explaining where the royalty income was reported.

Any youngster over the age of four that you claim as a tax dependent will have to have a social security number. The new law requires you to list it by the child's name when you file your 1987 return. Get the card as soon as you can. You won't want to procrastinate. The Social Security Administration expects that it will receive an extra 9 million requests for cards just because of this new rule.

Tax-exempt income will also have to be reported to the IRS beginning in 1987. The purpose is not necessarily to tax you. That's still not going to happen. The purpose is to give the IRS a true picture of your financial situation. An auditor may come to call and ask you where you got the money to buy the bonds that are generating your tax-free income. The IRS will want to make sure you originally paid tax on that income.

Estimated taxes are another money raiser. Instead of paying 80 percent of your taxes throughout the year so you wouldn't be penalized, the new law requires you to pay at least 90 percent. Fortunately, you can still pay 100 percent of last year's taxes, and still sidestep the underpayment penalty.

You have to pay your taxes or face a stiff penalty. It was one-half of 1 percent of the unpaid tax, up to a maximum of 25 percent. In the name of tax reform, it's just been doubled to a full percent, still up to 25 percent.

If you receive information about income and fail to report it on your tax return, you will be slapped with a negligence penalty. At Congress' urging, the IRS will be using this negligence penalty whenever possible. It used to apply only when a person forgot about dividends and interest income. But the new law is expanding that.

PART THREE

BRAND NEW TAX SAVING OPPORTUNITIES

True, the Tax Reform Act of 1986 overhauls the nation's tax laws, but that doesn't mean that every time-honored tax-cutting strategy and technique you've used in years past has been made obsolete. Many are as valid today as they have been for the past twenty years. For example, the interest you pay on your home mortgage is still fully deductible.

Other tax breaks, while they have lost some value, will still save you some tax dollars. The Individual Retirement Account is one example. Contrary to popular belief, you still have every opportunity to save on your tax bill. In fact, the new tax legislation provides new preferences to exploit, as well as new pitfalls to avoid.

In this section of the book, you will discover dozens of planning opportunities. You'll find everything from new year-end, tax saving strategies, to techniques that will allow you to pay for college for your children the tax-wise way. Critics say this can't be done, but they're wrong. You'll learn how to rethink your retirement planning, and find that you can still stash away a sizeable nest egg and defer taxes on the amounts you save. You'll find out why you should think in terms of starting your own small enterprise, devising new strategies for making charitable donations, and assessing investment opportunities, both in the securities market as well as in real estate. The savvy planner and investor can make himself or herself a financial winner by intelligently utilizing many of the most recent tax law changes.

17

Year-end tax saving plans

The last few weeks of 1986 offer taxpayers the unique opportunity to save what could amount to hundreds, perhaps even thousands, of dollars on their 1986 tax returns. All you have to do is act prudently before the end of the year. It's been a long time since taxpayers have had such an opportunity to save. But save you can. The fact is, you can profit handsomely from what the Tax Reform Act has done. Here's how.

The three years—1986, 1987, and 1988—are transition years. Each year, taxpayers will apply a different tax rate to income earned during that year. Each year, taxpayers will have a different set of deductions and credits to consider. So, by manipulating your income and tax preferences to your best advantage (keeping in mind the tax rates in effect for both the current and succeeding years), you can make sure that you don't pay any more tax than the law requires.

Following are dozens of potentially valuable year-end tax planning tips. Each is guaranteed to save you on your tax bill. Used in combination, they can save you a substantial amount of money. Just make certain that you give yourself enough time to implement each step of your tax-savings plan. Don't wait until the last week in December to put your plan into motion.

ACCELERATE YOUR TAX DEDUCTIBLE EXPENSES

Start with charitable contributions

Because tax rates are higher in 1986 than they will be in 1987, your deductions are more valuable this year. For example, consider making your charitable contributions to worthy organizations by year-end. In fact, make next year's donations, too. If you can afford it, make your gifts for three years. If you are in the top 50 percent tax bracket and make a $1,000 charitable donation in 1986, it will give you a tax benefit of $500. If you wait until January, 1987, that same $1,000 gift results in a tax benefit of $385. And if you wait until 1988 to make the donation, it's worth $280, reflecting the top tax bracket for each year.

If you've been planning to make a gift of valuable property, do it by year-end so you can get the maximum value out of it. A word of caution, however: when donating property valued at more than $5,000, you must get a reputable appraiser to look over the property prior to the date of the donation and attest to its value on IRS form 8283. You have to attach it to your return when you file. If you don't, your charitable donation deduction will be denied out of hand. So find your appraiser now. It can get hectic looking for a qualified individual a week before Christmas.

Pay your mortgage

Make certain you pay your December mortgage payment by year-end. Don't be late because you want the deduction in 1986 when it's more valuable.

Make state and local income tax and property tax payments

If you have not fully paid your state and/or local income taxes for 1986, get caught up. Make these tax payments by December 31. If you're not sure exactly how much you will owe, make your best estimate and get your check mailed by year-end. Do the same for any personal property taxes you might owe.

Medical bills should be paid this year

Say you have unpaid medical bills from visits to the doctor, the hospital, or the dentist; from the purchase of glasses, contact lenses, or hearing aids; or from medically-necessary travel, nursing care, prescriptions, and the like. If these expenses, when added to medical bills you've already paid this year, produce a total that will exceed 5 percent of your 1986 income (after insurance reimbursements), try to pay these bills by year-end. The idea is to load up on your medical expenses in 1986 if it looks like you'll qualify for the medical expense deduction because in 1987, only medical expenses that exceed 7.5 percent of your income (again, after insurance) will be deductible. As a practical matter, unless you suffer a long-term disability or catastrophic accident, chances are that you will never again be able to deduct medical expenses, assuming you have a reasonably comprehensive health insurance plan.

This is the last year for the sales tax deduction

After 1986, you will no longer be able to deduct sales taxes as an itemized expense. Typically, this doesn't amount to much, but all the deductions you can find are worthwhile. Most people use the sales tax tables provided by the IRS simply because it's too much trouble to keep track of every nickle and dime spent on sales tax during the year. Even those who use the IRS's table tend to cheat themselves on this deduction. The deduction is based on your adjusted gross income. Once that's established, you determine your deduction based upon the state you live in and the number of family members you have. But that's the mistake. You're allowed to add unreported and untaxed income to your adjusted gross. That includes a variety of items such as tax-exempt interest from municipal bonds, the untaxed portion of long-term capital gains (at least for 1986), and V.A. benefits. Frequently that extra income will boost your sales tax deduction.

In addition, there's a separate line on your tax return where you can deduct the sales taxes paid when you purchase a car, truck, boat, or plane. If you're planning to buy one of these items in the near future, do it now. Next year, you will lose the tax benefits of the sales taxes you've been charged.

Rethink your consumer interest payments

This will be the last year that you can fully deduct the consumer interest you pay on car, personal debt, bank, and other installment loans. The interest you pay on credit cards falls into the same category. Beginning in 1987, only 65 percent of your interest expenses will be deductible, and even that won't be as valuable as your interest deduction is this year. Remember, lower tax rates will be in force in 1987. So make plans now to reduce your installment debt. You'll receive very little benefit next year from interest charged by credit card companies, banks, and others.

Bunch your miscellaneous items into 1986

Load up now. Next year miscellaneous expenses will be deductible only to the extent they exceed 2 percent of your adjusted gross income. That means an individual earning $45,000 will have to incur $900 in these expenses before the next dollar is deductible. That same $900 is worth $315 in tax benefits, assuming a 35 percent tax bracket.

What kind of expenses qualify? Investment expenses, job hunting expenses, safety deposit box rentals, tax preparation fees, union dues, and the like.

Make maximum retirement plan contributions

That means fund your IRA. The maximum amount is $2,000 or 100 percent of your income, whichever amount is greater. If you are married and your spouse works, both of you can have IRAs for a family contribution of $4,000. If your spouse does not work, you can spread a $2,250 contribution between your accounts with no more than $2,000 going into one account, and no less than $250 going into the other.

Make your IRA contribution no later than April 15, 1987—the due date of your return. Make the contribution despite the fact that this may be the last time it's tax deductible. With the overall reduction in tax rates, the government is, in effect, saying that it is up to you to fund your own retirement years. The IRA may still be one of the best games in town because, after the Tax Reform Act takes effect, three out of four people will still deduct their IRA contributions.

If you are covered by a company-deferred compensation plan, put in as much money as you can afford. The top contribution for 1986 is $30,000. That drops to $7,000 in 1987. The same is true for a self-employed retirement plan; make the largest tax deductible contribution that you can afford.

DELAY INCOME INTO LATER, LOWER-TAXED YEARS

Why take income in 1986, risking taxation at relatively high rates, if you can receive it in 1987 or even 1988 at a time when rates will be much lower? Say, for example, you can choose when to receive a $5,000 year-end bonus or commission. In 1986 that bonus will put you in the 42 percent tax bracket. That means $2,100 of it goes to the IRS, while you get to keep the remaining $2,900. Some bonus.

By delaying that income to 1987, you will have that bonus taxed in, say, the 35 percent tax bracket. Here, the IRS will get $1,750. You save $350 in taxes by delaying the money for just a month or so. If you can get the bonus deferred until 1988, you can save even more. At that time the top tax rate will be 28 percent, so the tax on a $5,000 bonus is $1,400.

Now, you can't run away from income. That's illegal. You have to report your salary, wages, dividends, and interest income earned during the year. However, you frequently have the opportunity to schedule when you will actually collect bonuses and commissions. Discuss with your firm the idea of delaying this income until a later date. If you hold these discussions prior to the time you actually earn the money, you should be able to defer the income (and the tax) until 1988 when tax rates are much lower.

Self-employed individuals can bill clients so they receive their income when they want it. Delay billing until late December so you won't realize your income until January.

There is an exception to this notion of keeping your income down while tax rates are high. That exception arises when dealing with your investment income.

Sell profitable long-term investments by year-end, but hold on to your long-term losses; hold on to short-term profits, but sell short-term losses

That's pretty radical advice, but it's advice that can't steer you wrong. Tax rates on long-term investment profits will never be lower. (Long-term means that you have owned the investment for more than six months before you sell it. Short-term means that you have owned the property for six months or less. The distinction loses its bite in 1987.)

The top rate on long-term investment profits is 20 percent in 1986. In 1987, it jumps to 28 percent. And, in 1988 and later years, it can be as high as 33 percent. So, if you're sitting on a profitable investment that you've owned for more than half a year, sell by December 31, realize your profit, and pay tax on it. You can't go wrong.

About the only exception to this is when you have an investment that you intend to hold for the rest of your life. In that case, don't sell, but set it aside for your heirs who will inherit it at the date-of-death value, which is probably much higher than the price at which you acquired it.

The sell-now advice is for long-term profitable securities, not for short-term ones. If you sell the short-term in

1986, you could be taxed at rates as high as 50 percent. You're much better off waiting until 1987.

Also, you don't want to be in a net long-term loss situation when you file your 1986 taxes. That's because you only get a $1 write-off for each $2 worth of losses.

Take your short-term losses this year. They are deductible, dollar-for-dollar. The deduction will do you more good in 1986 when tax rates are generally higher.

If you think any of your profitable long-term investments are good ones, go ahead, sell and then immediately repurchase the security. There's no prohibition against that. The IRS does have a restriction called the "wash sale rule," but it only applies when you have an investment that you sell at a loss. In that case, you are prohibited from recognizing the loss for tax purposes when you repurchase the same security within the next month. But for profits, there is no wash sale rule.

18

Refinancing your mortgage

Thanks to tax reform, homeownership is more valuable than ever. It is one of the few true tax shelter investments untouched by tax revision. There are five excellent reasons to own your own home.

1. The interest you pay on your home mortgage, plus what you pay on the mortgage covering a second or vacation home, is tax deductible.

2. The real estate taxes you pay to the city or county are tax deductible, too. Although neither the real estate nor interest deductions are as valuable to you as they were prior to tax reform (because of the lower income tax rates), they still serve to reduce your taxable income. What's more, because of these two deductions, chances are you will be able to itemize other deductions such as charitable contributions, medical expenses, and other deductible taxes, making those expenses more valuable.

3. As your house appreciates in value over the years, you pay no immediate tax. You are only taxed on your appreciation in the year you sell. And if you purchase a more expensive place within two years of the time you sell the first house, the tax on the profit is deferred. Conceivably, you can avoid paying tax on the appreciation on your house forever.

4. Once you pass your 55th birthday, you can pocket, tax-free, as much as $125,000 of the profit from the sale of your personal residence. The rules are strict, but not too terribly difficult to overcome. For example, you can

only elect this deferral once in your lifetime. You must have occupied the house as your personal residence for three out of the five years prior to the sale. Your spouse, if you are married, must agree to the election. Things like that. Still, $125,000 tax-free is a lot of money. It is well worth it to watch all those details, which the IRS spells out on its tax form 2119, used for reporting the sale or exchange of a personal residence.

5. Your personal residence has just become your most important asset. It's your ticket into the new car show room. It is how your children will attend college. It is the wealth you want to tap when you need a loan.

Under the 1986 Tax Reform Act, Congress ordered that consumer interest should no longer be deductible. (Consumer interest is what you pay in finance and interest charges when you buy a car on time, carry credit card balances, or take out any type of installment debt, in general.) For 1986, consumer interest is 100 percent deductible. That drops to 65 percent in 1987, 40 percent in 1988, 20 percent in 1989, 10 percent in 1990, and is eliminated entirely in 1991.

The only exception to the loss of the interest deduction is for home mortgages. The obvious solution to borrowing is to tap home equity.

There are two reasons for homeowners to examine the wisdom of refinancing their home mortgages. The first reason is purely one of finance. You may be able to find a lower mortgage interest rate and more favorable repayment terms than you presently enjoy. The second reason is purely one of tax motivation. It makes more sense to pay interest that can be deducted than interest that cannot be.

If you pay interest on a credit card balance (presently running anywhere from 14 percent to as high as 22 percent), you will no longer be permitted to deduct that expense on your tax return. But if, instead, you have a line of credit at your bank using your home equity as collateral, you can go into that department store and write a check. Then as you repay your home equity loan (probably at 12 percent or so) you enjoy two benefits. First, you pay at a lower interest rate. Second, the interest is tax deductible.

So go ahead and refinance your home mortgage, or take out a second. It only makes sense to do so. However, as with most tax maneuvers, there are a few pitfalls to sidestep.

Watch what you have to pay for the privilege of refinancing. Loan closing costs can eat into the tax and financial savings. Look for the most favorable terms you can find.

Borrow only what you need. A line of credit makes the most sense. That way, you only have to repay what you actually need and use. It makes little sense to borrow $20,000 when you only need $12,000 for a new car. Also, keep in mind that you must repay what you borrow, even though it is your money from your home equity. Some people make that mistake, thinking that it's their money. It's the bank's, and don't you forget it.

If your home is worth, say, $160,000, and you owe $65,000, most lenders will let you borrow up to 80 percent of its value, less what you owe. That would be $63,000 ($160,000 times 80 percent, minus $65,000). Establish a $63,000 line of credit, tapping what you need, as you need it.

There's only one slight hitch. If you borrow against your home equity after August 16, 1986, you can only borrow as much as your original cost of the house, plus improvements you've made over the years. If you borrow more, then the interest you pay on the excess amount is not deductible.

For example, using the same situation as above, you paid $85,000 for your house originally, and added another $25,000 when you added a deck, fenced the back yard, and added an extra room off the porch. Your cost is $110,000. That's the most you can borrow and still deduct the full measure of your interest expense.

For most people this won't be a problem. But for some, it could be. Say, for example, you purchased a home years ago for $35,000, adding $15,000 to it over the years. You only owe $15,000. Your cost is $50,000. But now, because of the inflationary 1970s, the house is worth $175,000. Still, you can only borrow up to $50,000 if you want the interest to be fully deductible.

Typical of the tax law, there is an exception to the exception. First, Congress says that only mortgage interest will be tax deductible. Consumer interest is out. Then it rules that you can only borrow up to the amount of your cost in the property. Interest on excess borrowing is not deductible. Now, it adds this complication to the pot. There are three purposes for which you can borrow more than the original price of the house, plus improvements, and still deduct the interest. You can borrow to pay for medical expenses, educational costs (room, board, tuition, books, that sort of thing), and additional home improvements. Of course, it is up to you to prove to the IRS, should it ask, that you actually spent the funds on approved expenses.

There's a problem in a few states, such as Texas, that have homestead laws that prohibit a person from refinancing a personal residence to get at-home equity. There's not much you can do, except get the state legislature to reconsider. But if you can find someone to privately refinance your home, say your employer or a relative, go ahead. The IRS won't care. The refinancing will work in just the way it has been described here, despite state law to the contrary.

So, buy a home, and let it appreciate in value. Use it as your private bank. Write yourself a loan whenever the need arises, and continue to deduct the interest as you've always done. Try to avoid paying interest to credit card companies, on car loans, student loans, and other installment debts. With the loss of the tax deduction for consumer interest, it's just too expensive.

19

Planning divorce settlements

Look through the nearly 1,000 pages of the official version of the Tax Reform Act and you'll find no specific reference to divorce settlements. Yet, the effect of the law on divorce can be considered nothing less than profound. That's because of the combined effects of the higher personal exemptions, standard deduction, lower income tax rates, higher capital gain rates, and the phaseout of the personal exemptions and 15 percent tax brackets as incomes reach certain levels. Anyone involved in divorce proceedings needs to carefully review their expected tax situations in light of the new law because they probably are not what they seem at first glance. The harsh truth is—the entire equation has changed.

This much as not changed. Alimony is still deductible by the person paying it, and taxed to the person receiving it. The IRS wants names and social security numbers on the tax returns of those receiving the alimony to make certain that there's a match. Child support is not deductible by the person paying or taxed to the person receiving the check. It never has been, and hopefully never will be. Amounts received in property settlements are not taxed currently, but when the property is sold somewhere down the line, the person who sells is going to have to pay tax on the profit since the time the property was first owned. And finally, the personal exemption for children will go to the custodial parent unless there is a specific agreement calling for the child's exemption to go to the noncustodial parent.

Because of the dramatic cut in income tax rates, the ex- who has to pay alimony is going to be less anxious to send the check every month. The reason is obvious. The new law that puts the individual in a 28 percent tax bracket rather than a 50 percent bracket, also makes the price of the alimony payment almost twice as expensive as it once was. Say an ex-husband pays $2,000 a month in alimony and is in a 50 percent tax bracket in 1986. That translates to a $1,000 tax break every month, or $12,000 for the year. The alimony cost that comes directly out of his pocket is $12,000, not $24,000. But come 1988 when the top tax bracket is 28 percent, that same $24,000 annual alimony payment really costs him $17,280. So, when structuring a divorce settlement right now, keep that point in mind.

Also, the ex-spouse who is receiving the check will pay less tax on the money after 1986, again because of the cut in tax rates.

Some existing divorce decrees provide that they can be renegotiated when there is a substantial change in the law. You could argue that the 1986 Tax Reform Act constitutes such a change. You might want to go back into court and revise the alimony/child care formula so you wind up with the best situation you can. After all, there's no sense just giving your money to the IRS.

Future settlements will probably lean less heavily on alimony and more heavily on property settlements. Watch out. There's a trap that could be quite costly, perhaps years down the road. Say a divorced wife receives, as part of the divorce settlement, the family home. It's worth $180,000, but was purchased 20 years ago for $45,000. The appreciation is $135,000. There's no tax to pay until the property is sold. But when that happens, the wife is going to be saddled with tax on the full amount of the profit. That's because the long-term capital gains tax break ends January 1, 1987. All of the profit is taxed, although the top rate will be pegged at 33 percent, perhaps even lower, depending on other income.

And what about the personal exemptions for the children? That's always a hotly-contested issue among husbands and wives who are divorcing. Each exemption is worth $1,080 in 1986, soars to $1,900 in 1987, $1,950 in 1988, and $2,000 in 1989 and later years. The custodial parent will usually get to claim the deduction, unless the parties agree in writing to do otherwise. But how valuable is that exemption? If you can claim the full value of it, it can be quite valuable. But not everyone will be able to. In 1986 and 1987, the personal exemption for each of the children is fully available. However, in 1988 and later, that exemption can be reduced, depending on your income. Once it reaches certain levels, the benefit of the personal exemption is reduced. And, for single taxpayers and those claiming head-of-household filing status, those levels can be reached fairly easily.

So keep these ideas in mind as you structure, or even go back to restructure, your divorce settlements. Alimony payments made by an ex-spouse will not yield the tax breaks they once did. Alimony payments received by an ex- will not be as heavily taxed as they have been. It may be equitable to rethink the equation. There is no change in the child care formula. What's paid is not deductible; what's received is not taxed. Property settlements pose a problem for the appreciated property received because when it is eventually sold, that spouse will be responsible for the tax based on 100 percent of the profit. The elimination of the capital gains tax break is devastating. And finally, the personal exemption is substantially higher, but for those in the upper income brackets it may not result in any tax benefit, whatsoever.

20

New retirement thinking

Planning your retirement will take more time and effort than ever before. The enormously popular Individual Retirement Account (IRA) has been saddled with strict new rules and Keogh's for self-employed individuals are essentially unchanged. However, you cannot contribute to both in any one year after 1986, and rules covering company-sponsored retirement plans are significantly overhauled. The vesting period for qualified corporate plans is revised and amended, and federal employees and others will not be allowed to recover contributions to their retirement plans tax-free over the first three years of retirement.

Many in Congress argued quite eloquently that, because of the deep cut in personal income tax rates, individuals should be able to better provide for their own retirement needs than they have in the past, and that people should rely more on themselves and less on tax breaks to help them afford their later years. The bottom line result is that if you fail to adapt your retirement planning to the new situation caused by the 1986 Tax Reform Act, you face the very real possibility of going into retirement with money problems caused by a much smaller-than-expected nestegg.

Start your retirement reassessment with your IRA. Some 24 million workers across the country have set up and funded, at one time or another, their Individual Retirement Accounts. They are held at banks, savings and loans, credit unions, brokerages, and even insurance companies. About half are at local financial institutions, although more and more IRA holders are opting to direct their investments and are putting the funds into self-directed IRAs at their banks or into mutual funds.

The maximum tax deductible contribution to an Individual Retirement Account has been and remains $2,000, or 100 percent of your income, whichever amount is lower. A working husband and working wife can each contribute $2,000 for a total family deduction of $4,000. An individual with a nonworking spouse can contribute $2,250 into the family retirement fund, with no more than $2,000 going into one account, and no less than $250 going into the other. That's called a spousal IRA.

The rules on IRAs change dramatically beginning in 1987. So, for at least one last time, make your tax deductible IRA contributions for 1986. You have until April 15, 1987 to get your money into your account. Sorry, there are no extensions beyond that time frame, even if you get an extention to file your personal income tax return.

Here's what happens in 1987 and later years.

If you are single and not covered by a retirement plan at work, you can still have an IRA and deduct the contribution. The $2,000 maximim amount has not changed. Your retirement funds will accumulate tax-deferred over the years. Yes, if you invest wisely, you can retire as a millionaire. By all means, make your IRA contributions each and every year you can.

If you are single and covered by a retirement plan at work, and your income is under $25,000 before the IRA contribution is deducted, you can claim your full deduction on your tax return. Again, fund that account every year you can. It will grow and grow and grow.

If you are single and covered by a retirement plan at work, and your income is over $35,000, you lose the entire IRA deduction. Don't close your present IRA, but don't make a contribution even though you're allowed to make a nondeductible one. More on that below.

If you are single and covered by a retirement plan at work, and your income is between $25,000 and $35,000, you gain a partial IRA deduction. How much? In effect, you lose $1 worth of the deduction for each $5 that your income exceeds $25,000. Is it a good idea to make a partially deductible contribution? Perhaps. It depends on whether or not you anticipate needing the money prior to retirement, and how long you have until retirement.

If you are married and neither you nor your spouse are covered by a retirement plan at work, you can make a fully tax deductible contribution to each of your your IRAs no matter what your income. Only the $2,000 limitations mentioned above apply.

If you are married and either you or your spouse are covered by a retirement plan at work, you are covered as a couple under the following rules:

> If your combined income is below $40,000, you can make your IRA contributions and claim a full deduction just like under earlier law.
>
> If your combined income is above $50,000, you cannot deduct your IRA contributions.
>
> If your combined income is betwen $40,000 and $50,000, you can deduct a partial IRA deduction. Again, the amount that's deductible is reduced by $1 for each $5 worth of income above $40,000.

To spell out the question that's been raised by a number of people, what happens if a husband is eligible for a retirement plan at work, but he doesn't have vested benefits. In other words, he cannot collect a pension until he works there for at least five years. Can the family have an IRA even though their income is above $50,000? Answer: no. Just because the pension benefits are not vested is no excuse from the IRA rules.

That's all pretty simple. Just find the right slot, and you will know precisely whether or not your contributions to an Individual Retirement Account will be deductible.

What about people who have pre-existing IRAs? Should they stop making contributions if their incomes exceed those levels mentioned above? Yes, they probably should.

Does that mean you need to close out pre-existing IRA accounts? No, definitely not. Previously established IRAs should be retained. The dividends and interest accumulating in those accounts are still tax-deferred until withdrawn. If you close them out, you will be roundly taxed and penalized. There's no need for that. What's more, depending on how long you have until retirement, those funds will continue to grow.

But wait, there's still more. Not any great number of people will be precluded from making tax-deductible IRA contributions. According to the latest statistics available, three out of four people who presently have IRAs will still be entitled to a full IRA contribution deduction. Some 12 percent will be allowed a partial deduction. Only about 13 percent will lose the opportunity to deduct contributions to these retirement accounts.

But if you are one of those who lose the opportunity to deduct an IRA contribution, you should look elsewhere to set aside your money. An IRA is definitely not the place.

The law and conference reports point out that even a person who is denied a deduction for an IRA contribution is still allowed to make a nondeductible contribution if he or she wishes to do so. You lose the tax deduction, but any interest, dividends, and appreciation accumulate tax-deferred, until withdrawn. Even with that tax benefit, it's still a pretty poor idea, now that some of the details surrounding such a situation have come to light.

Say you are married and your income is above $50,000 a year. The law says you cannot deduct your IRA contribution. You make one anyway, even going so far as opening up a separate account so you won't co-mingle funds from your existing IRA with the new, nondeductible contributions. The idea is that the more you have in savings for retirement, the better off you are. That's true, but what happens if you need to tap into your IRA? If you withdraw funds prematurely from an IRA (before age 59 and one-half), you pay tax on the amounts withdrawn plus you pay a nondeductible 10 percent penalty. That's pretty stiff. You might think that you can get into the IRA money in the new account. After all, you didn't deduct anything. Surely the IRS wouldn't tax and penalize you for taking money from an account on which you've already been taxed. The committee report sheds some light. You will indeed be taxed and penalized on a pro rata portion of the amount of money in your combined IRAs. For example, say you have $8,000 in an IRA where you've deducted your contribution. You then add $2,000 in 1987 into a nondeductible IRA account. You need to withdraw $1,000 for some special need. According to the new plan, 80 percent of your IRA funds have yielded you a tax benefit, and 20 percent have not. Therefore, 80 percent of the amount withdrawn, or $800, will be taxed and penalized.

If you cannot deduct your IRA contribution, don't bother with such an account unless you are absolutely certain that you won't need to touch the money until you can withdraw it in retirement. That's as early as age 59 and one-half. But if you feel there's a chance you'll need the money, invest it instead in a tax-exempt municipal fund, a single premium whole life annuity, or even U.S. EE Savings Bonds. All can be redeemed when the money is needed. All make more sense than an IRA where the contributions are not deductible.

When it comes to vesting provisions, the tax law made some interesting and important changes. These provisions should make a difference to anyone who is considering a job change. Here's what the law says: Your employer has two options when it comes to setting limits on the retirement account it has for you. You must either be fully vested (entitled to your retirement) after working for five full years, or you must be 20 percent vested each year once you've worked at least three years. Under the second option, it will take you longer to be fully vested, but you'll at least be partially vested sooner.

That's important. For someone just starting a work career, you could work for as many as a half dozen companies over the next forty years. And you could be entitled to full pension benefits from each one. On its face, each may not be worth a tremendous amount, since pensions are typically based on length of service among other things. But combined, you could collect a sizeable amount each month.

So, when you consider leaving one firm for another, check the calendar. If it's just another month to six weeks before you complete another year, you might want to stay put. After all, your decision at the age of 35 could affect how much money you'll have to live on when you reach 65.

Soon-to-retire workers who have contributed to some of their retirement are not happy with a small change to the tax law. It was known as the "three-year rule." It said that if you helped contribute to your retirement fund and you could recoup your contribution within three years of your retirement, then you would pay no tax on the return of money you received. Once your contribution was all used up, the future amounts would be fully taxed. That rule is repealed, effective last July. Now, all retirees operate under the same rules. Any contributions are prorated. That means a portion of every pension check will be tax-free, and the remaining portion will be considered taxable income. It doesn't seem fair to change the rules in the middle of the stream for those workers who have counted on receiving up to three years worth of retirement benefits tax-free, but that is exactly what Congress has done. And, frankly, there's not one thing anyone can do about it.

There is one small consolation. In the long run, retirees are better off with the new rule. And with the tax rates slashed as they have been, the taxes on their pensions will not be as high as they would have been under old tax law.

It's interesting to hear so much these days about the latest restrictions on company-sponsored deferred compensation plans. The biggest, of course, is that employees will no longer be permitted to deflect more than $7,000 a year into one of these plans. The popular name is the 401(k) plan, named after that section of the Internal Revenue Code that authorizes it.

Still, if you think about it, $7,000 is extremely generous except, perhaps, for the person making well over

$100,000 a year. No matter how you cut it, $7,000 in deferred compensation is quite a bit of money to defer each year. It's certainly more than the $2,000 allowed for IRA contributions. Common sense says that the vast majority of workers covered by the increasingly popular retirement 401(k) plan have never had any intention of deferring more than $7,000 a year, even if they could.

If you have the opportunity to participate in a 401(k) deferred compensation plan, do so to the fullest extent possible. Remember, top tax rates will be highest in 1986 (50 percent), lower in 1987 (38.5 percent), and lowest in 1988 (28 percent). Deflecting income into later years only makes sense. But keep in mind that Congress always has the opportunity to raise rates in the years ahead. They will have to do something eventually to deal with the out-of-control federal deficit.

For example, if you can defer $7,000 from 1986 in a deferred compensation plan, and you are in a 50 percent tax bracket, you will save yourself $3,500 in tax this year. True, you will eventually be taxed on the money. But say it is in a year when the tax rate is a mere 28 percent. Then the tax will amount to $1,960. The savings is a whopping $1,540.

Go for 401(k) plans, and not only because of the tax deferral aspect. Employers typically pay interest on the amount of the deferred earned income that has been earned but not yet collected. This interest payment is a further boost to the desirability of these plans, since when you do get your money, it will be worth even more than what was originally deferred. What's more, the interest is usually paid at a higher rate than you could get in the open market today.

Self-employed individuals who have their own retirement fund, widely known as Keogh accounts, have not been terribly troubled by tax reform. The limitations on the amounts you can contribute have not been reduced or further restricted as under 401(k) plans. You can still contribute as much for 1987 as you do for 1986. You can still split your retirement money between profit sharing and money purchase plans. What you cannot do is have an IRA and Keogh in combination. Okay. Stick with the Keogh. It is much more generous.

Look for employers to set up more SEP–IRAs for their workers. That stands for Simplified Employee Plan–Individual Retirement Account. Under an SEP, the employer sets up the retirement plan, gets each employee to open up a personal IRA at his or her local bank or brokerage, and then makes the contribution on the workers' behalf. The benefit is twofold. First, it's easier and cheaper for an employer to administer an SEP–IRA and, second, the limitation is $7,000 a year for the employee, rather than $2,000 under a regular IRA. That's right— employees who have the money may put as much as $7,000 of their own money into an SEP-IRA each year. They just cannot have both the SEP and regular IRA contributions. It's your choice.

Take the advice of Congress. Plan for your own retirement because you can't rely on anyone else to do it for you. IRAs are probably less attractive than in the past, but it is likely that you also have more money to invest for your later years because of the latest tax law changes. Invest wisely because realistically, you can't expect social security benefits to provide a luxurious retirement. That's up to you.

21

Self-employment tax advantages

If you want to win the tax game (and, unquestionably, it is a game), start working for yourself. Now, I'm not suggesting that you immediately walk into your boss's office and tender your resignation. But I am urging you to listen to that inner voice that has been trying to get you to take that first step toward self-employment. More than 12 million people work for themselves across America. They will continue to profit by legally paying less tax than their employee-counterparts.

What can you do to earn a few extra bucks? Frankly, the opportunities are endless. You can turn what, up until this time, has been a hobby, special interest, or talent, into a money-making proposition. You can become a professional photographer, tutor, stamp collector or dealer, antique appraiser, or clock repairman. You name it, and you can make money at it. Start part-time if you want. Encourage an at-home spouse to begin work at home. Not surprisingly, you may find that what starts out on a shoestring turns out to be a very big deal in the year ahead.

But be professional. Keep up-to-date with your business books and records, listing all of your business income and, of course, your tax-deductible expenses. Give receipts when people pay you. Ask for receipts when you pay people. File the proper tax forms and pay your taxes on time. There's nothing worse than getting behind with the IRS.

Put in a business telephone line. Open up a separate business bank account. Advertise in local journals. Hire an accountant at least to set up a decent recordkeeping system that will satisfy the IRS, should one of its auditors come to call. Set out a calendar of what tasks need to be performed at what time of the year. None of these are absolute requirements, but they go a long way toward establishing a professional business attitude.

The tax law is chock full of tax breaks for the entrepreneur. And what's more, the new tax law does very little to change those advantages.

Net self-employment income is still taxed, but at much lower rates than before. Your net self-employment profits are included in your personal income, with the top tax rate in 1988 and later years pegged at 28 percent. In 1986, you could pay up to 50 percent of your business profits to the IRS. In 1987, that drops to 38.5 percent.

The cost of doing business is still deductible. That means you can deduct the cost of accounting services, legal fees, utilities, taxes, operating expenses, business transportation, 80 percent of your business meals and entertainment expenses (that's new, it used to be 100 percent), salaries and wages paid to employees, retirement plan contributions, and more.

You can still travel, attending business conventions, meetings, and seminars. The cost is deductible so long as the purpose of the meeting is directly related to your trade or business.

You can travel to and attend your business's annual meeting.

You can still depreciate your Mercedes, although not as rapidly as before. You cannot take the investment tax credit (it was repealed retroactively to January 1, 1986), but you can deduct up to $10,000 a year in equipment and other depreciable materials you purchase.

You can still drive on business, and deduct the cost of operating your vehicle, just like you always could.

Interest paid by your business on purchases it makes, such as for the cars it finances, is tax deductible, while the consumer interest that individuals pay is not fully tax deductible. Let your business foot the bill so you can take advantage of your business tax status.

By my mind, the self-employed individual has it all over the corporation. If you're just starting a business, don't bother to incorporate. It's too costly from a tax standpoint. And if you are already incorporated, you may want to investigate the possibility of unincorporating, or at least electing subchapter S tax status for your business operations. Subchapter S of the Internal Revenue Code provides that a business can legally operate as a corporation, but for tax purposes, all of the business's profits and losses are passed through directly to you, the business owner. The corporation itself pays no income tax. Since individual tax rates will be lower than corporate rates, that's the smart way to go.

Small corporations will have to set a fiscal year that corresponds to the calendar year, unless a corporation's officers can provide the IRS with convincing arguments that another fiscal year is more appropriate. The possibility is exceedingly unlikely. The IRS likes businesses to be on a calendar year. It makes things easier to administer. This will mean that most existing small corporations will have to adjust their tax years to the January-December time frame sometime during 1987. This will mean a costly visit to the accountant. It's not clear what would happen if the IRS would deny you permission to change.

The reason behind this switch to the calendar year for most small businesses is that Congress no longer wants small business owners to be able to juggle income and deductions between various tax years to their tax advantage.

By not incorporating or unincorporating, or electing subchapter S status for your business operations, you will pay tax on your business profits only at your personal income tax rate.

It's precisely because operating expenses are tax deductible that the self-employed individual gets far more tax breaks than the employed worker. Remember, the individual loses his deduction for sales taxes. But the businessman doesn't. If he buys a typewriter for $1,000 and pays 4 percent sales tax on it, he can just lump that sales tax in with the purchase price for depreciation purposes. True, he loses an immediate deduction, but in the long run he gets to deduct it from his income.

A major tax savings results from the miscellaneous itemized deductions that individuals will find next to impossible to claim, but that businessmen will still enjoy. Beginning in 1987, the price tag of such personal itemized deductions as tax preparation and advice, safety deposit box rentals, investment fees, and union dues, will only be deductible to the extent they exceed 2 percent of a person's adjusted gross income. That means for a person making, say, $50,000 a year, the first $1,000 worth of these expenses will not be deductible. Only amounts exceeding that level can be written off.

But for the businessman, those costs are part of operating the enterprise. The business needs its tax return filled out. It has to pay the bank the fee for a safety deposit box to hold business records and business investments. The business's investments need to be handled, and any fees and charges associated with those will be deductible, too. The price of business publications, professional journals, dues, and other subscriptions paid by the business will be deductible without regard to that 2 percent limitation.

Small business operators don't have to resort to cheating. They still have a great many opportunities to save on their taxes without resorting to fraudulent activities. Report all your business income because the law requires it, and it's the right thing to do. Then, when it comes to your business operations, make a profit and pay tax on it, although you don't want to pay more than the law requires.

For example, pay your spouse a reasonable salary for the work he or she performs for your business operations. The business gets to deduct the salary, which you report on your joint tax return. It's a wash. So what's the point of the exercise? You do not have to pay social security or unemployment tax on salaries paid to a spouse. That means the money is subject to neither self-employment taxes nor social security taxes. That alone is a terrific savings.

If your net profits are below $40,000 a year, both of you are eligible for IRAs. Or better yet, cover yourself and your spouse under the business's retirement plan. That way you can put away much more than $4,000 a year.

Hire your children to work in your office. Exactly what they do depends entirely on the type of buisness you have and what their interests are. For example, a child who is a bit of a computer whiz may be the ideal person to help in computerizing your files. The issue has been long decided, since a judge ruled that a father and mother who ran a small trailer court were being miserly when they only paid their seven-year-old son the minimum wage. Pay your kids what they are worth, and deduct the amounts on your Schedule C when you file your taxes.

The children, in the meantime, will have to report their wages and salary when they file their returns. If their income is under a couple of thousand dollars a year, they won't have to pay any income tax. Terrific. The W-4 withholding form tells you when they don't have to file. Make them fill out a form and sign it. That way, you won't even have to withhold any income taxes. What's more, there are no social security taxes due on wages paid by a parent to a minor child. Again, that's quite a tax savings. You get the deduction, and the child gets the income tax free because he earns less than a set amount.

You may have heard that children under the age of 14 have to pay tax on their income at their parent's highest marginal tax bracket. That's true, but it only applies to unearned income, not earned income, such as wages and salary. You can pay your children all you want (as long as the amount is reasonable for the work performed), and not fall within this tax trap that affects unearned income.

There are changes that the self-employed individual, even the part-timer, should know. The so-called hobby loss rules have been modified. Under earlier law, if you were profitable in any two out of five consecutive years, the IRS presumed you to be serious about your business.

If you were not profitable to that degree, the IRS was free to challenge you, saying you weren't really in business, but rather were trying to write off the expenses associated with a hobby or some other activity not engaged in for profit.

The new rule says that you need to be profitable at least three out of five consecutive years. This slightly tougher restriction goes into effect January 1, 1987.

But that's okay. You should be profitable anyway, or at least try to be. And even if you are not, as long as you try to run your operation, even on a part-time basis, in a business-like manner—keeping books and records—you should be able to successfully defend your operating losses.

Home office expenses are still tax deductible against your business profits. Additional expenses that can't be deducted during the current tax year can be carried forward to be applied against the business income of the next year. If they can't be utilized that year, continue to carry them forward until they can be used.

22

Tax breaks that have not been repealed, and a few that have

Contrary to popular belief, not every tax break that you've ever used has been wiped off the books by the 1986 Tax Reform Act. The fact is, not only have many survived tax reform, but some are more valuable than ever. Certainly, some tax breaks have been repealed, but others have been only slighted modified. What's more, most of the tax law changes, whether repealing or revising various sections of the tax law, are effective as of January 1, 1987. That's important to keep in mind as you put your tax plans into effect.

Only a handful of tax provisions are affected retroactively. The businessman's favorite, the investment tax credit (ITC), is repealed as of January 1, 1986. The tax benefits of Clifford and spousal remainder trusts are eliminated for all new trusts established after March 1, 1986; pre-existing trusts are fine. Just don't add any new assets to them. New pensioners who leave work after June 30, 1986 and who contributed a portion of their retirement fund, will no longer enjoy the benefits of the so-called "three-year rule"; that allowed you to recoup your pension contributions tax-free within the first three years after you retired. When refinancing a mortgage after August 16, 1986, don't refinance more than the original price of the house plus improvements. If you do, the interest on the excess borrowing will generally be considered consumer interest, and consumer interest is phased out as a deduction beginning in 1987. Those are the main items that have retroactive application. As a rule, you can plan that the tax law changes brought about by the Tax Reform Act will become effective in 1987 and later.

Not every tax break has been changed, however. Here's a sampling of what's still good, and a few that have only been revised.

Medical expenses are still deductible under the same terms and conditions as earlier law. The only significant change is that, beginning in 1987, you need to pay out 7½ percent of your income in medical bills before the next dollar is deductible. The 1986 level, of course, is 5 percent. The cost of capital improvements to your house to accommodate someone who is ill or handicapped remain tax deductible, just as under earlier law.

State and local income taxes are still deductible by itemizers for the year in which the payments are made.

Real estate taxes as well as personal property taxes are deductible, too. The only "tax" deduction that has been repealed is that for sales taxes.

Mortgage interest you pay is deductible, as is the interest you pay on a second or vacation home. If you sell one vacation home and buy another during the year, that's fine. The interest on both are deductible because you only held one at a time.

Charitable contributions will still be deductible under the same rules as those which held prior to the latest tax law changes. The only difference is that nonitemizers lose their ability to claim their generosity. But that's not because of the tax act. Nonitemizers were scheduled to lose the charitable donation deduction under prior law.

Casualty losses remain deductible to the extent they exceed 10 percent of adjusted gross income, after insurance reimbursements and $100 per loss. There is one important change here. The new law requires that if you have insurance coverage, you must file a claim and at least try to get the insurer to reimburse you for your loss. Prior to this change, many people were willing to forego filing a claim, especially for smaller accidents and mishaps for fear that the insurer would cancel their policies.

Miscellaneous itemized deductions are still available, but have undergone limitation beginning in 1987. The new rule says that your miscellaneous deductions must exceed 2 percent of your adjusted gross income before the next dollar will be deductible. This restriction effectively ends this deduction for most people. Included in this group of expenses are fees you pay for unreimbursed employee business expenses, tax return preparation and advice, safety deposit box rentals, union dues, the cost of small tools, job hunting expenses, investment advice and fees, and so forth.

The valuable tax credit for child and dependent care is retained under the new law without modification.

You can still deduct the cost of a job-related move, but beginning in 1987, the price tag for moving expenses must be taken as an itemized expense deductible from your adjusted gross income, rather than a straight deduction against your gross income. The distinction is important. You will now have to itemize in order to take the moving expense. Through 1986, you did not have to itemize, but only had to file the long form.

Gambling losses are still deductible up to the amount of your gambling winnings. With so many people playing state-run lotteries these days, this deduction is showing up on increasing numbers of tax returns.

Alimony paid by you continues to be deductible. Alimony received by you continues to be included in your income. Child care is neither deductible by the person who pays it, nor taxable to the person who receives it.

Business gifts you make to an individual are deductible by the firm as long as the price tag is $25 or less. There's no change to this long-standing rule.

Along the same lines, you still don't absolutely have to keep receipts for business meals and other items when they amount to under $25 in order to get credit for these business expenses on your tax forms. Nevertheless, it's still a good idea to keep those receipts, even for small amounts, since they will help prove your expenses should the IRS audit your return.

The usual expenses associated with operating a business enterprise remain tax deductible. What you pay in salary, taxes, utilities, accounting and legal fees, and other operating expenses, are tax deductible.

If you use your vehicle in your trade or business, or operate it as an employee for your firm, you can still take either the IRS optional standard rate of 21 cents a mile, or your actual operating expenses, including depreciation.

Parking fees and tolls are deductible in addition to the operating expenses of a car when it is driven on business.

Depreciation is still a valuable deduction, although for most new cars, equipment, and real estate, the rules have changed substantially. The depreciation system that was in effect when you purchased and placed in service your old equipment remains the system you should continue to use for that particular equipment.

Depreciation on business autos is limited to $2,560 for the first year, $4,100 for the second, $2,450 for the third, and $1,475 for each succeeding year until the price of the car is recovered.

Individual Retirement Account contributions will still be deductible for three out of four taxpayers, according to the latest statistics. Another 15 percent or so will be able to claim a partial IRA deduction for their contributions to their retirement accounts.

Amounts you contribute to your Keogh retirement plan are tax deductible so long as you stay within the legal limits.

There's still a great deal of tax-free, or only partially taxed sources of income.

Federal tax refunds are tax-free.

State and local tax refunds, when you did not itemize the year before, are tax-free.

The interest on most tax-exempt municipal bonds is also tax-free. Watch for special activity bonds. Some of the interest may be subject to at least the minimum tax povisions.

Scholarship and fellowship grants continue to enjoy their tax-free status, but only when the funds are used to cover tuition costs and course equipment.

Workers compensation payments and veterans' disability benefits are tax-free.

Gain on the sale of your home is tax-deferred when you replace it with a more expensive residence within two years of its sale.

Up to $125,000 of the profit from the sale of your personal residence is tax-free as long as you have passed your 55th birthday when you sell, have used the property as your personal residence for at least three out of the past five years, and meet a few other specific requirements.

Interest, dividends, and capital appreciation collected in your retirement accounts (IRAs, Keoghs, 401(k)s) is tax-deferred until withdrawn in retirement.

Life insurance proceeds are not taxed.

Up to $5,000 in employee death benefits remains tax-free.

You can receive a gift without paying tax on it.

Inheritances and bequests you receive are free of federal income tax.

If you want to make a gift, you can give as much as $10,000 a year before even reporting the gift transaction to the IRS. Husbands and wives can jointly make gifts totalling $20,000 before involving the IRS.

Just as before, there is no gift tax on transfers between a husband and a wife.

Estates of decedents dying in 1986 valued at up to $500,000 are not subject to estate taxes. Estates of decedents dying in 1987 or later valued at up to $600,000 are not subject to estate taxes.

The interest, dividends, and capital appreciation that accumulates in a single premium whole life annuity are tax-deferred. This is one of the better tax breaks around since the 1986 Tax Reform Act.

Series EE Savings Bonds have the same tax benefits that they've had for years. Tax on the interest can be deferred until the bond is cashed.

Investors in U.S. Treasury Bills continue to receive a neat little tax break. Interest (actually the technical term is original issue discount) isn't taxed until the year the bill matures, rather than the year the bill is purchased.

Business travelers can continue to tack on personal vacations to legitimate business trips, and still deduct the cost of the business portion of the trip.

Business owners can and should hire their spouses and children to work in their operations. Social security taxes are not due on wages paid to a spouse and minor children by a sole proprietor.

While children will be taxed at their parents' highest marginal tax rate on income generated by assets transferred to them by their parents and others, that rule only applies when the child is under the age of 14. Parents can still transfer income-producing assets to youngsters age 14 and up.

23

New strategies for charitable giving

The latest changes to the tax law argue forcefully for you to develop new strategies for your charitable giving.

Scheduled increases in the standard deduction for 1987 and 1988 will produce fewer individuals who will itemize their deductions. That will hurt the level of charitable giving because, by law, 1986 is the last year that itemizers will be allowed to deduct their donations. The drop in the income tax rates in 1987 and again in 1988 will hurt, too, because those charitable contributions that can still be deducted will be made that much less valuable.

Those individuals donating appreciated property to worthy organizations may find themselves subjected to the tougher minimum tax because of their generosity.

Due to these and other changes made to the tax law by the 1986 Tax Reform Act, many of the nation's largest and most reputable charitable and similar organizations are frantic for your donations, especially this year. Churches, synagogues, colleges and universities, the Heart and Cancer funds, Goodwill, the Salvation Army, and others are all fearful that, because of changes to the tax law, people will just stop giving or give smaller amounts, especially individuals who have been used to the tax benefits of giving gifts to charities.

Personally, I don't think that will happen. Americans have always risen to the occasion when there's been a need, whether or not a tax benefit is made available to them. People will give to the needy just as they always have, simply because it's the right thing to do. But the big givers will think twice about the tax effect of their gifting program.

Here's the effect tax reform is expected to have on gift-giving, and what you might consider doing about it.

If you are planning to make charitable contributions in this and future years, dig extra deep into your pocket before the end of 1986 if at all possible. Consider the possibility of doubling or even tripling your donations this year. If it's not possible to come up with the extra money in 1986, you'll still be better off making the lion's share of your donations in 1987 than in 1988. (Caution: Keep your charitable contributions down to no more than 50 percent of your income. Remember, there are various limitations on the amount of gifts you can deduct, and you probably don't want to exceed them. The general limitation is that you can deduct no more than 50 percent of your income in charitable contributions in any one year. Unused amounts can be carried over to future years. But remember, tax rates are lower in future years, so the deductions won't do you as much good.)

If you've been thinking of eventually donating that piece of real estate to your alma mater, or an antique silver tea set to your church, or those corporate stocks and bonds to the local YMCA, or your valuable collection of Civil War artifacts to the local museum, get going on your plans. Don't tarry.

All of this hectic activity points directly to the dramatic cuts to personal income tax rates. Make a $5,000 charitable contribution in 1986 when your tax bracket is, say, 42 percent, and you will enjoy a tax benefit of $2,100. If you wait until sometime in 1987 to make that gift, your tax benefit will be worth only $1,750 if your top marginal tax bracket is 35 percent. And if you wait still longer, until 1988 or later when the personal tax rate peaks at 28 percent, your tax benefit will be a mere $1,400. Give now when rates are highest. Income tax brackets are highest in 1986, not quite as high in 1987, and still lower in 1988. That means your deductions will do you the most good in the year that the brackets are highest.

For someone earning $50,000 a year, you can generally contribute up to $25,000 worth of money and property to tax-qualified organizations, and enjoy an immediate tax deduction for your efforts. If you have any doubt as to whether or not your donations will be deductible, ask for clarification either from the officials of the organization receiving your gift, or at your local IRS office. The IRS has a book, *Publication 78,* that lists each and every organization that is qualified to receive your tax deductible contributions.

Even if you aren't in the major leagues of charitable giving (say you can only afford to give $300 a year), charities still value you and your gift. You should consider upping the amount of your gifts at the end of 1986 in order to get the most out of your charitable donations.

For anyone planning to give valuable property to a charitable group, get started lining up a reputable appraiser. They become terribly busy toward the end of the year when others just like you have the same idea about boosting their charitable donations. The IRS has a relatively new rule that requires anyone who plans to donate property valued at more than $5,000 to hire, at their own expense, an appraiser of high professional standing. This appraiser cannot have been involved in the deal when the property was obtained (either by gift or purchase) and cannot be involved with the group that will be getting the property. The appraiser must sign IRS Form 8283 attesting to the property's value in his or her opinion. You have to attach that completed form to your tax return when you file in April. If you don't hire the appraiser and don't bother to attach the completed form to your return, you lose your entire charitable contribution deduction that's based on your gift. Period. No exceptions, says the IRS.

At least the cost of the appraiser is deductible in 1986 as a miscellaneous itemized deduction. In 1987 and later years, miscellaneous deductions are restricted to amounts that exceed 2 percent of your adjusted gross income.

The tax law throws a curve at those making donations of appreciated property. It's called the minimum tax, and if you're not careful, it could cause you a nasty (read costly) surprise.

The tax law has long subjected certain individuals to the minimum tax. These are the people who have effectively avoided paying tax on most of their income through various tax loopholes and special preferences.

Congress didn't think that was fair, to say nothing of the people who pay 25 percent or more of their income to the IRS. So they passed a rule that intends that everyone pay at least something. The minimum tax rules provide that everyone should compute their income taxes two ways. First, you go through the regular system, where you add up all your income, subtract your deductions and personal exemptions, and apply the applicable tax rate. Second, under the minimum tax system, you add to your regular income certain other items that have not previously been subject to income tax. These are called "tax preference" items. From this total, you subtract an exemption amount ($40,000 for married couples filing jointly; $30,000 for singles; $20,000 for marrieds filing separately), and from this result apply a 21 percent tax rate. You pay the higher of the two results.

Most people don't have to worry about the minimum tax because they don't have enough tax preference items to concern themselves. But there are new items on the list, thanks to tax reform, including one that affects charitable donations of appreciated property.

Prior to the tax law change, anyone who owned property that had gone up in value over the years could donate it to a recognized charity, deduct its fair market value, and not pay any tax on the appreciation. Pretty good deal.

You can still do that, and it's a good idea if you are not damaged by the minimum tax. See, now you will have to include as an item of tax preference the amount of untaxed appreciation allowed as a charitable contribution deduction for purposes of computing the minimum tax. If you have any concern that the minimum tax might cause you problems, discuss its impact with a knowledgeable tax professional prior to the time you transfer your gift to the charitable organization—not afterwards. By then it will be too late.

The bottom line is this: Give generously, especially this year when your gift will do you the most good. If you donate valuable property, have an appraiser look it over before you transfer it to the charity. And if you give appreciated property, consider the impact of the minimum tax before you finalize the gift.

24

Assessing investment opportunities

The 1986 Tax Reform Act has turned the investment world on its ear. It seems as though everyone is chock full of advice on what's likely to go up and what's likely to drop in value. The truth is, no one knows for certain. No one is quite sure exactly what to expect from stocks and bonds, real estate, oil and gas, municipal bonds, even lowly U.S. Savings Bonds, once the full impact of the tax law takes effect. And, frankly, that won't be for a couple of years. But this much is certain; this Tax Reform Act certainly has every investor's undivided attention.

CAPITAL GAINS—GONE, BUT NOT FORGOTTEN

The highlight of tax overhaul is the extraordinarily deep cut taken in personal income tax rates. Remember, after all was said and done, the overall effect of the tax bill was to be revenue neutral, neither raising nor reducing taxes. So, to counter the revenue drain caused by the drop in individual tax rates, Congress decided to eliminate the investor's favorite—long-term capital gains. Capital gains, in one form or another, had been part of the tax code since 1921, so the repeal is really a dramatic move. Nevertheless, it is repealed.

Effective Janaury 1, 1987, 100 percent of your net investment profits will be included in your income. No longer will an investor be granted the privilege of selling an investment at a profit, pocketing 60 percent of his gain tax-free, and registering only the remaining 40 percent as income.

What's more, the distinction between long-term and short-term ends at the same time. You will no longer have to consider the calendar when thinking of selling an investment. All investment profits and all investment losses will be treated equally no matter how long you owned an investment before selling.

The top capital gains tax rate in 1986 is 20 percent. That's the 40 percent of investment profits that are subject to tax, multiplied by the top 50 percent personal income tax rate.

Still, that's significantly lower than what you might pay in 1987, where the tax rate on net investment profits will top out at 28 percent, even though 1987's individual income tax rates will reach a high of 38.5 percent.

In 1988 and beyond, net investment profits will be fully taxed just like any other type of income. If you are in the 28 percent tax bracket (the highest official rate at that time), you will have to turn over 28 percent of your stock market gains to the IRS. If your income is high enough so that you lose some or all of your personal exemptions and the benefits of the 15 percent tax bracket, the rate of tax on your net investment income could conceivably reach 33 percent.

I keep mentioning "net" investment profits because profits from investments will still be used first to offset any losses you may suffer in the market. You will simply add up all the investment profits you realized during the year, and subtract the amount of investment losses you suffered. If you enjoy a net profit, you will be fully taxed on it. If, on the other hand, you suffer a net investment loss, you will be allowed to deduct up to $3,000 of it. You will have to carry forward to future years any unused investment losses that you currently cannot use. You will then apply the unused investment losses first to future investment profits, and then to the $3,000 annual limit just mentioned.

The smart move is to recognize your investment profits in years when the tax rates on them will be lowest. So if you have the opportunity, sell your profitable investments in 1986 while the long-term capital gains tax break is still on the books. The tax rate will never be lower. Hold on to long-term capital losses until 1987 or later. In 1986, only half of your net long-term losses are deductible, and then only up to $3,000. If you sell at a loss in 1987, all of it will be deductible. In essence, it may become twice as valuable.

While personal income tax rates are cut, first in 1987 and then again in 1988, the tax rate on investment profits does just the opposite. It increases. For 1986, long-term capital gains taxes on investments amount to no more than 20 percent of your profits. Of course, that's the maximum. Chances are you actually pay capital gains rates far below 20 percent since the maximum rate only reaches individuals in the top 50 percent tax bracket. And, frankly, few people find themselves in such heady company. In 1986, a single taxpayer won't pay 50 cents on the dollar on his salary and other regular income until his income exceeds $88,270. A married couple filing jointly won't reach the 50 percent tax bracket until their combined taxable income exceeds $175,250. Only the top echelon of American households have incomes that exceed $50,000 a year.

So, realistically, most people find themselves in, say, the 36 percent or 42 percent tax bracket for their taxable incomes. Say your 1986 marginal tax bracket is 42 percent. That means your capital gains tax rate is 16.8 percent. (That's 42 percent times the 40 percent of your investment profits that are taxed.) In 1987, that tax rate will soar to 28 percent even though your total income may not. That is quite an increase.

So, in almost every situation, you will benefit over the long haul by selling profitable investments in 1986 and recognizing your profits for tax purposes. If you still like the investment you just sold, buy it back. You can do that. Go ahead and call your broker, sell your 100 shares of XYZ Corp, and in the next breath, tell your broker to buy back 100 shares of the same corporation. Sure, you'll have to pay transaction costs (so use a discount broker who charges the lowest fees), but you'll lock in your profits at the lowest rates you are likely to see in your lifetime. Yes, Congress could go back in a year or two and increase tax rates. It's unlikely that the capital gains tax preference will be reinstated.

Don't make the mistake of thinking the IRS will prohibit this kind of deal. It's fine with the tax agency. What they don't like is when you sell an investment at a loss and then repurchase the same investment within the next month. That's called a "wash sale." Wash sale losses are not recognized for tax purposes.

There are only three exceptions to the advice of selling profitable investments by the end of 1986. First, if you plan on holding the investment until your death, don't sell. Let your heirs get the property at the date-of-death value. Second, don't sell when the fees and commissions are just too expensive to swallow, or the time frame for selling is too long. A prime example would be an apartment building you own. And third, don't sell when you anticipate taking investment losses next year or the year after. You may want to save some of your profits to use as an offset against those losses when the time is appropriate. After all, no tax (when you use the offset) is better than a 20 percent tax rate.

For the millions of investors who own equity mutual funds, you may want to effect a telephone switch if you belong to a fund family. Call in and tell them to switch your portfolio from their equity fund into their money market fund and then back into the equity fund. There's usually no or very little charge for intrafamily transfers. You lock in your taxable gain since mutual fund transfers are considered sales and purchases to the IRS.

STOCKS AND OTHER EQUITIES

Many Wall Street watchers are anticipating a great deal of volatility during the last few months of 1986. Even though institutional investors move the market these days, there are still enough small individual investors around who will be making year-end sales (and probably repurchases) to cause significant market movement. It's not the perceived value (or drop in value) of a stock issue that will move its price, but rather the cause and effect of tax reform. Things should settle down after the first of the year.

That's not to say that some stocks won't benefit mightily because of the tax overhaul bill. Some companies in particular and industries in general are net winners under tax reform. Others are losers in the truest sense of the word.

The biggest winners are those firms that received special consideration from Congress behind closed doors. The biggest losers are those that didn't receive the special favors but still must compete with others in their industries.

The winners received unique treatment under what's commonly referred to as "transitional rules." There are literally hundreds of these rules sprinkled throughout this new law. Congress used to call them "Christmas tree" giveaways, but now that's too obvious. You can't tell from reading the new law who exactly is helped. The technical language hides the identities quite well. But the laws are so narrowly drafted that the tax benefits can only help one particular taxpayer. For example, while many projects are in peril because of new restriction of private activity bonds, a few special exceptions are carved out where these bonds will still carry tax-exempt interest.

Another broad example of favoritism is the oil and gas industry, versus real estate. Oil and gas received special consideration and help from Congress. The reason is that key legislators were from states that will benefit from the extra aid and the Committee chairmen needed their votes. Real estate, on the other hand, had no vocal champion, and it was here that Congress came down the hardest. Oil and gas is a relative winner under tax reform. Real estate is one of the biggest losers.

Others destined to be winners are the consumer-styled businesses. The price of their stocks should go up. That includes media firms, producers of household products, food, and other retailers (because people will have money to spend), among others.

Still other corporate winners should be those firms that have been burdened in the past with a high corporate tax. Since taxes have been cut for big businesses, those firms should receive a windfall. That will probably be reflected in corporate stock prices, and certainly in corporate dividends.

There's another side of stock investments to consider. Are you looking for growth, income, or a combination of the two? The change in the tax law repealing the tax break for capital gains is one that changes the equation for growth stocks. An 8 percent growth rate on a stock that pays no dividend is no better than a stock that languishes but pays an 8 percent dividend. Keep that in mind as you reassess your stock portfolio.

This holds true for equity mutual funds. If your fund is not performing up to the level of others that invest in income rather than growth, you might want to consider changing.

BONDS

Many consider bonds to be a particularly good buy right now, especially tax-exempt municipal bonds. But don't ignore utility bonds, high-grade corporate bonds, or even Treasuries.

The thinking is that when people start pulling what little money they can get out of their tax shelters, they will probably sink it into bonds. The question is, what kind.

Tax-exempt municipal bonds, muni-bond funds, and municipal unit investment trusts are among the very few places left where a person can get tax-exempt income. At least through 1987 when personal tax rates can be as high as 38.5 percent, tax-exempt income will remain a high priority for many investors. However, when rates drop to 28 percent in 1988, owners of municipals may want to rethink their investment strategies. Depending on interest rates, they may be able to do better (after taxes) with high grade corporates or even Treasuries than with municipals.

As things stand right now, municipals are a good buy. Rates are quite high when compared with corporate bonds or Treasuries, especially with personal tax rates at the level that they are.

Part of the allure of taxable bonds instead of tax-frees, of course, is the lower personal tax rates. You won't be paying nearly as much tax on your interest under the new tax law.

TAX SHELTERS ARE OBSOLETE

Let's face it. What Congress gave, it has now taken away. Tax-sheltered investments are only a distant memory for many people. But for others, they are still a terrible headache.

Congress has simply ordered that you can no longer deduct tax losses generated by your investment in tax shelter limited partnerships against regular income, such as your salary, wages, interest, dividends, and the like. Well, that's not exactly true. Losses from shelters purchased after August 16, 1986 cannot be deducted against regular income. Losses suffered in 1986 from shelters purchased earlier will still be 100 percent deductible that year, 65 percent deductible in 1987, 40 percent in 1988, 20 percent in 1989, 10 percent in 1990, and finally will be totally nondeductible in 1991 and later.

So what can you do with limited partnership tax shelter losses? About the only alternative is to find similar investments that generate a profit, and then use that profit to offset the losses.

The key here is the word "passive." Tax shelter limited partnerships are defined as passive investments, and Congress has decreed that losses from these and other passive investments shall not be deductible, but can only be used to reduce gains from these and other passive investments. They cannot be used to offset profits from "active" investments. And that puts a crimp into tax shelters.

It's obvious that if you are sitting with these losses, you should be actively seeking out passive investments that throw off profits. Fortunately, there are some opportunities.

Real estate, by definition, is a passive activity, with but one limited exception (see chapter 25). Investments in stocks and bonds are considered active investments, even though you may turn over your entire portfolio to someone else to handle for you. (You can't get more passive than that, but it's still considered an active investment activity.)

Many people who, in the past, have participated in limited partnerships will be aggressively trying to sell their interests. Many are required to continue paying into them for five years or more. It's a legal obligation, and one that the general partner will be all too willing to enforce. Investors will have to sink good money into shelters that generate unclaimable losses. And they can't just walk away and ignore their financial obligation. As a result, savvy investors may be able to find deals that make good financial sense at bargain basement prices. When the price is right, you may be able to take what would otherwise be a losing proposition and turn it into a money maker.

What's more, there are a growing number of syndications being made available that will be profitable right from the start. They may not be absolutely terrific deals from a profit standpoint right now, and you may be better off investing your money at less risk and higher return elsewhere, but at least you will be doing something to bail yourself out of a tenuous tax shelter investment situation.

There's one more point about tax shelter losses that owners and investors should keep in mind. Even though you won't be allowed an immediate direct benefit from losses you have taken in these investments, you will be able to claim your losses when you eventually sell. That's when everything is finalized for tax and accounting purposes.

REAL ESTATE INVESTMENT TRUSTS

Better known as REITs, these investments have escaped tax reform unscathed. They bear looking into. A REIT is much like a mutual fund, only it invests in a pool of commercial properties. Most REITs pay healthy dividends, and with the best REITs you will find that your investment appreciates in value. You purchase shares in a REIT through an investment broker, just like you would buy shares of stock in a corporation.

The beauty of a REIT is that it pays no tax. It makes its money by investing in real estate, and then distributes its profits to its shareholders. It develops property, and rents it out. A REIT is not in the business of buying and selling properties, but rather looks to develop and own them. That provides for a great deal of stability. A REIT can sell no more than five properties a year and must hold a property for at least four years before selling.

SINGLE PREMIUM WHOLE LIFE INSURANCE

Here's a tax shelter that has survived reform, even though no one expected it to. It is looking better all the time, especially for those who are frozen out of Individual Retirement Accounts.

Single premium whole life is a form of long-term savings. It's packaged by insurance companies to take advantage of something very important—the tax deferral that protects life insurance earnings from immediate income tax.

You can put $10,000 into a single premium whole life policy with a guaranteed yield of, say, 8 percent for the next five years. After that, the yield will vary in line with market interest rates. Typically the guaranteed yield will be a percentage point or more than what is being paid by a solid municipal bond fund which, by the way, is just as fully sheltered from federal income tax.

But, while bonds fluctuate in price as interest rates rise and fall, these don't. A $10,000 investment is always worth $10,000, plus, of course, the accumulated earnings.

About your earnings. You can take them in cash, or let them accumulate and compound. You can also withdraw some of the principal if you want.

There are disadvantages. You can't cancel the policy or cash it in entirely. If you do, you will have to pay income tax on every penny you ever received under the policy.

Especially after the new tax law which restricts so many other investment opportunities, a single premium whole life policy makes a good investment if you're looking for secure tax-free income and are willing to let most or all of your initial investment pass to your heirs.

The fact is your heirs will receive not only what you invested, but also the life insurance protection part of the policy.

U.S. TREASURY SECURITIES

These still make a lot of sense, especially Treasury Bills. The interest (or original issue discount) paid on Treasury investments is not taxed at the state or local level. Plus the tax rate at the federal level will be lower than at any time in recent history.

The third benefit is peculiar to Treasury Bills. They provide a terrific technique for shifting income from one year into the next. All you have to do is select the maturity you need to accomplish your goal. Say you are reading this in November, 1986. You can withdraw $10,000 from your bank account and send it to the Bureau of the Public Debt or one of the Federal Reserve Banks that sell Treasury Bills. You buy a three-month Treasury, maturing the first of February, 1987. The result is that you have transferred two months of 1986 interest income into 1987. That's because the law says when you have a Treasury Bill that matures within a year of the time it was issued, you have to declare the interest income in the year the bill matures, not the year you receive the interest. When you purchase a Treasury Bill, you send in $10,000, and then within a few days, the Treasury Department credits your account with the amount of your interest (technically called original issue discount). You get your $600 interest almost immediately (in 1986) but won't have to pay tax on it until you file for 1987 (when tax rates will be lower.

The savvy saver will be buying one-year Treasuries in Janaury and February, 1987 in an effort to get the interest income immediately, while deferring the taxable income intil 1988 when tax rates will be lowest.

SERIES EE SAVINGS BONDS

The once lowly United States Savings Bond has become the recent darling of the little investor. As this book is being prepared, these $25 bonds are paying 7.5 percent when held to maturity. That takes five years. Seven and one-half percent looks pretty good these days. And if rates go back up, you can expect these savings bonds to increase their rates, too. The rate is geared to a formula based on what U.S. Treasury bills pay.

The interest is free from state and local income taxes. The interest can accumulate in the bonds tax-deferred until withdrawn. In fact, they can be converted to HH bonds and used as a retirement fund.

SAVINGS ACCOUNTS

If you're holding long-term certificates of deposit, you look like a genius. Some outstanding long-term bonds (outstanding in more than one sense) are still paying 12 percent or more. With the cut in personal tax rates, you will enjoy more of your money than ever before. The saver is definitely helped by tax reform because he won't have to turn over nearly as much of his interest to the IRS at year-end. Those long-term certificates are good investments to have and to hold, especially when they are yielding a high rate of return.

This is the time to reassess your investment options. Look through your portfolio with a critical eye, keeping in mind the tax law changes that have already affected, and will affect in the future, all of your stocks, bonds, mutual funds, savings accounts, certificates of deposit, and other investments. Keep in mind the severe drop in personal income tax rates to come in the years ahead, as well as the elimination of the long-term capital gains tax break. Realistically assess the opportunities for your investments to increase in value based on what the new tax law has done to particular companies and industries. Then, make your move. And be quick about it, especially as the end of 1986 approaches.

25

Real estate tax planning

If you listen to the doomsayers, you'll never consider real estate as a tax saver again. So, don't listen. For most people, real estate is still a superb tax-cutting investment vehicle despite what others might have you believe. Certainly it is not as enticing as it once was, but then nothing is. Not even fully tax-exempt municipal bonds are what they were, so why would you expect real estate to get through tax reform without at least a few scratches?

If you are not a homeowner, become one. If you can't afford it, save until you can.

If you can swing it, start investing in local townhouses or separate unit residences, and lease them to others. The time is certainly right, with interest rates being as low as they are and bankers being flush with cash to lend on worthwhile projects. Real estate is still a safe investment as far as bankers are concerned because they always have the property to back up the loan. Just make sure, when you invest in that home or townhouse, that you are directly involved in the management of your property holdings. More on that in a minute.

START YOUR REAL ESTATE EMPIRE WITH YOUR OWN HOME

The law has divided taxpayers into two classes—those who own their homes and those who don't. The law encourages people to own rather than rent by providing owners with wonderful tax incentives that just are not available to renters.

Owners can deduct the mortgage interest they pay on their primary personal residence as well as what they pay on a mortgage covering a second or vacation home. If you have a beach or mountain property that you use for family trips, you can deduct the mortgage interest on the loan that covers it. If you sell it and purchase another, you can deduct the interest on that loan, too. What's more, you can deduct the real estate taxes you pay on those properties. Those two deductions—mortgage interest and real estate taxes—combine to create a terrific tax saver that is simply unavailable to renters.

These two deductions enhance your other itemized deductions. Because the standard deduction is scheduled to jump to $5,000 for married couples beginning in 1988, Congress expects fewer people to itemize. This will mean that if you own a house, you'll itemize the deductions associated with it, plus others as well. If you rent, chances are you won't be able to itemize. And if you can't itemize, you can't take any tax break for your charitable contributions, other tax payments, a portion of your consumer interest, or miscellaneous deductions.

Moreover, full interest deductions are restricted to what you pay on your home mortgage loan. I've mentioned the rules before, but they certainly bear repeating. Consumer interest is what you pay on your credit card balances, student loans, bank borrowings, car loans, and other installment debts. For 1986, all of that interest is tax deductible as an itemized expense. However, in future years, the deduction is limited. For 1987, only 65 percent is deductible, 40 percent in 1988, 20 percent in 1989, 10 percent in 1990, and none of it in 1991 and beyond.

Fortunately, as a homeowner you have an alternative that renters do not. You can tap into your home equity, use that money to pay outright for items that you would ordinarily purchase on time, and deduct the interest on the home equity loan as you repay it.

Say, for example, you want to buy a car for $15,000. Your house is worth $200,000 and you only owe $46,000 on it. Your banker is anxious to extend a line of equity credit for you to use at your discretion. So, instead of financing the car (and not being able to deduct the interest you would pay on the car loan), you borrow against the equity in your house and pay cash for the automobile. At tax time, you can deduct the interest you had to pay to the bank because the loan covers your home.

There is a limit to the amount you can borrow from the bank on your home equity and still deduct the interest payments. But it is not terribly restrictive. The rule is this: you can borrow no more than what the house first cost you plus the price of improvements you have made to it over the years.

So, if your home cost you $68,000 and you have added a deck, fence, and finished off the basement at a cost of another $22,000, your cost basis would be $90,000, while you may only owe $40,000. If, today, your house would sell for $175,000 in the open market, your banker would probably be willing to lend you as much as $100,000. That's 80 percent of the fair market value of the house, less the outstanding amount of your mortgage. But according to the law, you are looking for trouble if you borrow more than $90,000, the cost of the residence plus improvements.

Actually, there are three exceptions to this restriction. You can borrow more than your cost basis if you use the extra funds to pay for medical bills, educational expenses, and, of course, more home improvements.

What happens if you borrow more than you're allowed, and don't use the funds for one or more of those three purposes? You just cannot deduct the interest you pay on that portion of the loan.

Realistically, most people aren't ever going to want or need to borrow $100,000, or the $90,000 maximum allowed in this example. In fact, most won't use this equity loan device except for reasonably small amounts, such as to buy a car, pay for vacations, furniture, or other big-ticket items.

Use your home equity wisely. Don't borrow more than you want or need, because you must pay it back. It may be your home equity you're borrowing against, but keep in mind that the loan must be repaid.

Consider the pros and cons of refinancing or taking out a second mortgage loan to pay off an outstanding debt on which consumer interest is being charged. And don't wait because the longer you do, the more nondeductible interest you'll have to pay. The purpose of refinancing is obvious and twofold. Pay the home equity loan so the interest portion will be fully tax deductible, instead of paying with a credit or bank card, or other financing where the interest will be only partly deductible. Also, a home equity loan will usually come in at an interest rate that is well below what you would pay on other types of consumer debt. It is certainly much lower than what you pay on credit cards. So, not only are you keeping a full tax deduction for consumer interest, but you are also reducing your overall cost of borrowing money. That's perhaps the biggest plus of all.

There's no question about it. Homeownership has it all over renting, except if you are the landlord.

LANDLORDS ENJOY THE BEST OF BOTH WORLDS

Once you own your home, you should consider the benefits of buying one, two, or even three pieces of rental real estate. The investment and tax benefits can be wonderful, although not quite what they were before tax overhaul. Then they were outstanding.

Newly-purchased residential real estate must be depreciated over 27.5 years using the straight line method. That means you get a depreciation deduction worth 1/27.5 every year you own the property and use it for rental purposes. If you owned residential rental property before the law was changed, you should continue using the same depreciation method that was in effect at the time you acquired the house. That may be 15, 18, or 19 years on an accelerated basis.

If you purchase commerical as opposed to residential property, you need to depreciate it over 31.5 years, again on a straight line basis.

Okay, so the depreciation deduction isn't as terrific as it once was. It's still not horrible, especially when you consider that the property is appreciating in value rather than deteriorating. That's what a depreciation allowance is supposed to cover—the wearing out of an asset.

Another plus to owning rental property is that you can watch it appreciate in value over the years and you won't have to pay a dime's worth of tax on that increase until you sell. There is still no immediate tax on an asset you purchase and hold.

When you do sell, you lose the benefits of long-term capital gains tax rates.

Now, here's where the real tax advantages come in. Under the Tax Reform Act, real estate activities are defined as "passive" in nature. That means you have to add up all your rental income from your property for the year and subtract your operating expenses (repairs and maintenance, real estate taxes, mortgage interest, assessments, and the like) as well as depreciation. If you end up with a profit, you have to report it and pay the corresponding tax at the prevailing rate. But if you are operating at a loss, you cannot deduct it. Losses from passive investments can only be offset against profits from passive investments. Congress has tossed real estate investments into the same pot as limited partnerships where you don't have a part in the active management of the investment. So, with your rental real estate activity, you either need to operate at a profit or have some other source of profitable passive income to offset the loss. If you don't, you will have to carry over the loss to a future year when you have those profits, or take them when you eventually sell the property.

AN IMPORTANT EXCEPTION

There's an exception important to the small real estate investor who is actively involved with his or her property. This exception won't apply to the person who simply turns over all the details of the property management to an outside firm.

If you are active in the management of your real estate rental properties (fixing leaks, approving tenants, painting walls, that sort of thing) and your income is under $100,000 a year, you can deduct up to $25,000 worth of losses a year from your rental properties. If you have more than $25,000 in losses, the excess can be offset against "passive" income or else carried over to future years when it can be used. If your income is above $150,000, you cannot deduct any of your real estate losses. If your income falls between $100,000 and $150,000 annually, you can deduct a portion of your losses.

That's an important exception, especially for the small real estate baron-to-be who starts out with one or two townhouses. You'll find that over the years, you can build up quite a bit of equity in your properties. What's more, as rents increase, you will find that you develop a positive cash flow. It won't be too many years before you are operating at a profit, and when that happens you won't mind paying income tax on your annual gains.

Index

Accounting, 32
Accrual method, 32
Alimony, 113, 133
Amortization, 31
Appraiser, 139
Averaging
   income, 5, 42–43
   ten-year forward, 23–24
Awards, 6, 44

Benefits
   unemployment, 5–6
   veterans' disability, 134
   See also Compensation
Blind, 4, 5, 41–42
Bonds, 148–49
   municipal, 20, 69–70, 72, 134
   Savings, 63, 135, 143, 153
   tax-exempt, 19–20, 69–73, 134, 148
Business, 29–32, 87–93
   small, 89–90
Business conventions, 30, 48–49
Business entertainment, 30, 47–48, 89
Business meals, 30, 47, 89

Business travel, 30, 48–49, 136

Calendar year, 32, 84, 93, 127
Cancer fund, 137
Capital gains, vi, xii, 11, 55–58, 143–46
   corporate, 31–32, 87–88
Capital losses, 145
Cars, luxury, 31, 92
Carter, Jimmy, 89
Casualty losses, 10, 52, 132
Charitable contributions, 45
Charitable deductions, 7, 61, 132, 137–41
Charitable travel, 8, 48
Charities, 137–41
Child care, 133
Children, 42
   and Social Security numbers, 35
   under and over age fourteen, 26–27, 136
Child support, 113
Churches, 137
Clifford trust, vi, 25, 26, 83–86, 131
Coins, gold and silver, 22, 80

162 / Index

Compensation
  plans, deferred, 22, 23, 81
  unemployment, 39, 43, 134
  See also Benefits
Compliance rules, 33–36, 95–97
Conferences, business, 30, 48–49
Congress, v, vi, 15, 33
Consumer interest, 50, 104
Contracts, federal, 35
Contributions, charitable, 45
Conventions, business, 30, 48–49
Corporate capital gains, 31–32, 87–88
Corporate minimum tax, 32, 92–93
Corporate tax rates, 29, 87–88
Corporations
  personal service, 32
  S, 32

Deductions
  charitable, 7, 61, 132, 137–41
  depreciation, vi
  expensing, 31
  itemized, 7, 44–45, 49–53, 103, 137–41
  medical expense, 7, 45–46, 103, 132
  miscellaneous itemized, 9, 49–50, 104, 133
  standard, 4, 40–41
  two-earner, 5, 42–43
Deferred compensation
  plans, 22, 23, 81
Delay income, 105–7
Dependent care, 133
Depreciation, 16, 58–59, 65–66, 90–92, 134
  deductions, vi
  for property, 30–31
Dividend exclusion, 12, 88, 89
Dividend pay-outs, 29, 89
Divorce settlements, 113–15

Educational travel, 8, 48
Elderly, 4, 5, 41
Employee benefits expenses, 7–8
Employee business expenses, unreimbursed, 8
Employee fringe benefits, 10, 52–53
Entertainment, business, 30, 47–48, 89
Equities, and stocks, 67, 146–48
Equity, 158
Estates, 25, 83–86
Estimated taxes, 35, 84
Exemption, personal, 4, 5, 41–42
Expenses
  medical, 39
  tax deductible, 102–5
Expensing allowance, 90–91
Expensing deductions, 31

Failure to pay, 34
Family and estate planning, 25–27, 83–86
Faulty information, 33
Fellowships, 6, 43–44, 134
Fraud penalties, 34, 71
Fringe benefits, employee, 10, 52–53

Gambling losses, 133
Gifts, 61, 133, 138
Gold coins, 22, 80
Goodwill, 137

Hardship withdrawal, 23

Heads of household, xii, xiii
Health insurance, 10, 52–53
Heart fund, 137
Historic restoration, 59
Homes, 9, 135, 155–58
  See also Mortgage
House of Representatives, viii, ix, x
House Ways and Means Committee, viii, ix
Housing benefits, 7

Income, delay, 105–7
Income averaging, 5, 42–43
Income shifting, 26, 85–86
Indexing, to inflation, 5
Individual Retirement Account (IRA), vi, 21–22, 23, 50, 75, 76–80, 91, 99,104–5, 117–24, 134, 135, 151
Individuals, 3–10, 39–53
Inflation, 5
Information, faulty, 33
Information reports, to IRS, 34, 96–97
Installment payments, 14
Insurance
  health, 10, 52–53
  life, 13, 14, 61, 151–52
Interest
  bond, 70–71
  consumer, 50, 104
  mortgage, 9, 50–52, 132
  and municipals, 20, 69–70, 72, 134
  paid to IRS, 34, 95
  tax-exempt, 19, 20, 35
Internal Revenue Code, v
Internal Revenue Service (IRS), 1, 19, 20, 25, 32, 33, 35, 70–71, 91, 139

Investment opportunities, assessing, 143–53
Investments
  long-term, 106–7
  and tax changes, 11–14
Investment seminars, 8
Investment tax credit (ITC), 16, 30, 64–65, 66, 90, 131
Investors, 17, 55–61
IRA. *See* Individual Retirement Account (IRA)
IRS. *See* Internal Revenue Service (IRS)
ITC. *See* Investment tax credit (ITC)
Itemized deductions, 7, 44–45, 49–53, 103, 137–41
  miscellaneous, 9, 49–50, 104, 133

Keogh retirement plan, 21, 76–80, 117–24, 134, 135
Landlords, 158–59
Laws, tax, new concepts, v-vii, 131–36
Life insurance, 13, 14, 61, 151–52
Local taxes, 6, 44–45, 102, 132, 134
Long-term investments, 106–7
Long-term losses, 106–7
Losses
  capital, 145
  casualty, 10, 52, 132
  gambling, 133
  long-term, 106–7
  short-term, 106–7

Married couples, xii, 3, 4, 22, 40, 42
  See also Married taxpayers

Married taxpayers, 39, 40, 42
  See also Married couples
Meals, business, 30, 47, 89
Medical expense deduction, 7, 45–46, 103, 132
Medical expenses, 39
Military, 7, 46–47
Minimum tax, 20, 59–61, 72–73
  corporate, 32, 92–93
Minimum tax provisions, 13–14
Ministers, 7, 46–47
Miscellaneous itemized deductions, 9, 49–50, 104, 133
Mortgage, 102
  refinancing, 109–12, 131, 132
Mortgage interest, 9, 50–52, 132
Moving expenses, 8, 49
Municipal bonds, 20, 69–70, 72, 134

Negligence penalties, 34

Overseas workers, 10, 52

Packwood, Robert, ix, x
Partnerships, 32
Penalties, new, 33–34, 35, 71
Pensions, 23
Personal exemption, 4, 5, 41–42
Personal residence, 9, 58
Personal service corporations, 32
Personal tax rates, 39–40
Political contributions tax credit, 7, 46

Prizes, 6, 44
Property taxes, 6, 44–45, 102, 132
Publication 78, 139

Rates, tax. *See* Tax rates
Reagan, Ronald, v, vii, ix
Real estate, 61, 67–68, 147
  and depreciation, 58
  tax planning, 155–60
  and tax shelters, 17
  transactions, 34–35
Real estate investments, 12
Real estate investment trust (REIT), 13, 150–51
Real estate taxes, 6, 44–45, 102, 132
Refinancing, mortgage, 109–12, 131, 132
Rehabilitation expenditures, 12–13
REIT. *See* Real estate investment trust (REIT)
Renters, 155, 156
Reporting, to IRS, 35
Residence, personal, 9, 58
Restoration, historic, 59
Retirement, and three-year contribution rule, 24
Retirement planning, 21–24, 75–82, 104–5, 117–24, 135
Rostenkowski, Dan, viii, x
Royalty payments, 35, 96

Sales taxes, 6, 44–45, 103–4
Salvation Army, 137
Savings accounts, 153
Savings Bonds, 63, 135, 143, 153
Scholarships, 6, 43–44, 134
S corporations, 32

Securities, United States Treasury, 152
Self-employed, and Keogh retirement plan, 21, 76–80, 117–24, 134, 135
Self-employed workers, 10, 52–53, 125–30
Senate, viii, ix, x
Senate Finance Committee, ix
SEP-IRA. *See* Simplified Employee Plan-IRA (SEP-IRA)
Series EE Savings Bonds, 63, 135, 153
Settlements, divorce, 113–15
Shifting, income, 26, 85–86
Short-term losses, 106–7
Silver coins, 22, 80
Simplified Employee Plan-IRA (SEP-IRA), 23, 75, 81, 117–24
Single taxpayers, xi, xiii, 3, 4
Small business, 89–90
Social Security, children's numbers, 35
Social Security Administration, 96
Spousal remainder, 85
Standard deduction, 4, 40–41
State taxes, 6, 44–45, 102, 132, 134
Stock market, 67, 146–48
Stocks, and other equities, 67, 146–48

Tax
  brackets, xiv, 5, 7–8
  deferral, and personal residence, 9
  estimated, 35, 84
  laws, new concepts, v–vii, 131–36
  minimum, 20, 59–61, 72–73
  planning, real estate, 155–60
  rates, 5, 25
    corporate, 29, 87–88
    1987, 1988, and later years, x–xiv
    personal, 39–40
    slashed, 3–4
  rate schedule, 83–84
  saving plans, year-end, 101–7
  shelters, 15–18, 63–68, 149–50
    investors penalized, vi, 35
  See also specific tax
Tax deductible expenses, accelerate, 102–5
Tax-exempt bonds, 19–20, 69–73, 134, 148
Tax-exempt interest, 19, 20, 35
Tax Reform Act, v, vi, x, 1, 11, 29, 37, 39, 45, 61, 63, 99, 131–36, 143
Ten-year forward averaging, 23–24
Time table, of tax reform, vii-ix
Trademark costs, 31
Trade name costs, 31
Transitional rules, 147
Travel
  for business, 30, 48–49, 136
  charitable, 8, 48
  educational, 8, 48
Treasury, United States. *See* United States Treasury
Trusts, 25, 83–86

Two-earner deduction, 5, 42–43

Unemployment benefits, 5–6
Unemployment compensation, 39, 43, 134
United States Treasury, vii, viii, 15
  Bills and securities, 152
Unreimbursed employee business expenses, 8, 49–50

Vesting, 81–82
Veterans' disability benefits, 134

Wages, and tax shelter losses, 16–17
Whole life policies, 13, 151–52
Workers
  overseas, 10, 52
  and pensions, 23
  self-employed, 10, 52–53, 125–30

Year, calendar, 32, 84, 93, 127
Year-end tax saving plans, 101–7
YMCA, 138
Youngsters' Social Security numbers, 35

Zero bracket amount, 40–41